The
Teachings of
Yogi Bhajan

The Teachings of Yogi Bhajan

Siri Singh Sahib Bhai Sahib Harbhajan Singh Khalsa Yogiji

HAWTHORN BOOKS, INC.
Publishers/NEW YORK

THE TEACHINGS OF YOGI BHAJAN

Library of Congress Catalog Card Number: 76-56526
ISBN: 0-8015-7461-7
1 2 3 4 5 6 7 8 9 10

Prayer

Thou Infinite One, it is Thy grace, the highest opportunity for humanity that we can sit and think and be together to praise thee, O Lord. O creative consciousness, O cosmos, moment of positive existence, positive relationship, positive love and brotherhood, dedicated unto this, the highest reward on this planet for the individual being, and You are the one who granted it. Our gratitude for this, and may your blessings shower upon us to make us healthy, happy, and holy, and may we live in a raised consciousness of universal consciousness of love, peace, and harmony. Give us the power to exalt thee. Give us the power to be thy channel in existence of the Holy Nam.

Sat Nam

Contents

Preface

This book has been written with one intention: to take people from a negative state of mind to a positive one. The sentences have been constructed with a special permutation and combination to cut the negative thought waves and to trigger the positive polarity in the human mind. The thought wavelength has been reproduced and lies within these lines to turn the negative into positive.

All the words are based on the principle that "In the beginning was the Word, and the Word was with God and the Word was God." And all the sentences have been worded in such a way as to work on the Heart Center (compassion), the Throat Center (to improve communication), the Third Eye (Ajna) and thus open the person's intuition, and the Thousand Petalled Lotus (Sashra) to purify the thoughts.

The words in this book are themselves a complete meditation. They should be read like a Gospel for this book contains the hidden science of Nadh, the science of eternal sound. The words have been spoken from the consciousness of a Mahan Tantric, for which privilege I, as a human being in this time and space, am grateful to God and Guru Ram Das.

The Teachings of Yogi Bhajan

Introduction:
Sa-Ta-Na-Ma
Meditation

"In the beginning was the Word. And the Word
was with God. And the Word was God."
The Gospel according to St. John

Every element of the universe is in a constant state of vibration manifested to us as light, sound, and energy. The human senses perceive only a fraction of the infinite range of vibration, so it is hard to comprehend that the *Word* mentioned in the Bible is actually the totality of vibration which underlies and sustains all creation.

A person can tune his own consciousness into the awareness of that totality with the use of a mantra. By vibrating in rhythm with the breath to a particular sound that is proportional to the creative sound, or sound current, one can expand one's sensitivity to the entire spectrum of vibration. It is similar to striking a note on a stringed instrument. In other words, as you vibrate, the universe vibrates with you.

By practicing a mantra, you can raise your awareness of yourself and your environment and work constructively to improve both. The mantra that I teach is Sat Nam (Sa Ta

3

Na Ma), which means: Truth manifested. This mantra of Sat Nam was given by Guru Nanak, the first of the Ten Sikh Gurus, over 475 years ago. It is composed of five primal sounds which are proportional in their combined vibration to the totality of creation. *Sa* means totality, *Ta* means life, *Na* means death, and *Ma* means resurrection. The fifth sound is the *ah* sound which is common to these four. It is the creative sound of the universe.

As you chant, the thumbs are touched to each fingertip in rhythm with the mantra in order to channelize the energy through the nerve endings in the finger which are connected to the brain centers relating to intuition, patience, vitality, and communication. On the sound of Sa touch the thumb to the first finger, with Ta to the second finger, Na to the third, and Ma to the fourth.

Chant the mantra in three ways: out loud, in the voice of the human being; whispering, in the voice of the lover; and in the silence of your own consciousness, the voice of God. From the depth of your silent meditation, come back to the whisper and then to the full voice. Throughout the meditation, each syllable of the mantra should be projected mentally from the back top of the head, down, and then straight out the third eye point, which is located between the eyebrows at the root of the nose.

Sit in a comfortable posture with your legs crossed. Keep the spine straight. Chant the mantra out loud for five minutes; whisper for five minutes; and then silently meditate, internally repeating the syllables for ten minutes. Again chant in a whisper for five minutes and then five minutes out loud. Now, inhale and stretch the arms up. Hold the position and exhale. Inhale again, exhale again. Relax. The total time will be thirty-one minutes.

Using this technique, you can experience your own infinity. Exceeding the limitation of your own worldly experience, you can know the Unknown and see the Unseen.

If you spend two hours per day in meditation, God will meditate on you the rest of the day.

Word

T he time is now and now is the time.   1

T he greatest mantra of this age is *keep up*.   2

T he highest, most effective energy on this planet is the   3
word. There is nothing beyond it, there shall be nothing beyond it, and there was nothing beyond it; therefore, we
must consciously understand the power of the word. When
we understand the power of the word and we apply the
whole mind behind the word, then we create the word
which can create the whole world for us.

O ne who does not know how to live to his word does not   4
know how to live. And happiness will never come to him,
because the word was with God, the word created this
world. But if you will honor the word, you will be honored
in this world.

The subconscious mind acquires a certain imagination; 5
from that imagination comes a steadfast altered state of
consciousness which time cannot wipe out. This is why the
first wise words, the word of God given to man was, "I am, I
am." And man is such a fool that he only remembers half of
it. "I am, I am" means I am because I am, because of the
existence of I am, I am a creature because of the Creator. "I
am, I am." God and me, me and God are one. That's what
it represents.

Without power to speak, without power of silence, if you 6
can become powerless at this moment perhaps He may answer faster than you think. Allow your mind to become
meditative, clean yourself. Neither the body, nor your
possessions, nor you will remain forever; therefore, beginning with this moment, for an entire day, utilize your energy
gracefully to perceive the unperceivable, hear the unheard,
and see the unseen. It is He who is unseen, but you are a
part of Him and He is a part of you. Try consciously offering
your body, your mind, and your soul. He may accept, He
may not accept.

Today your beauty lies in the acceptance of the principle 7
which doesn't accept any principle. Become shelterless, let
everything go; reduce yourself to nothingness, work on
your mind, and pressurize it down and down and down and
down to the realization of nothingness. I was, I was not, I
am, I am not, I shall be, I shall be not. All is yours, glory is
yours, nature is yours, surroundings are yours, the world is
yours, I am yours, all to the unknown, ever to the unknown. Levitate your consciousness to total nothingness. I
was not, I am not, I shall be not. Do not let your mind
betray you, because your mind and your soul must at this
time unite together.

8

Where is the guru? Everywhere. When somebody 8
speaks the truth to you, that is a guru. Forget about who is
speaking. The true word, the true vibration, the true signal
is the true guide.

The facts of teachings often are distorted through rituals 9
and time, when people who know those teachings do not
live them as their life experience.

What was the basic word? There are seven primary 10
sounds in which all the effective vibratory music of man is
recorded: Sa, Re, Ga, Ma, Pa, Da, Ni; that's all. In these
seven sounds, all the music of the whole universe and communication is recorded and written. Out of these seven
primary sounds, five are primal sounds. In those five primal
sounds comes one primal word which was in the beginning,
which is now, and which ever shall be.

Words should never be routine. Words exist in the in- 11
finite beginning of each person. With words you make
friends, with words you contract yourself, with words you
can slander people, with words you can praise people, with
words you can become almighty, with words you can become just useless. Every word you say has a vibration that
brings you what you have and what you need. So be very
careful when you speak a word, because one word spoken
can make and mar the destiny of the being. In the beginning
there is a word, but when you put your heart into it, the
word becomes a totality, love; when it is without heart, it is
lust.

A stage will come when you can hear the unheard, see 12
the unseen, know the unknown. What change there will be
in your personality and in your life, in your behavior and in
your existence on this planet, and in the contentment and
joy and happiness you can experience; words cannot explain because that will be your experience. Candy is sweet.
How sweet? I can't say. The one who has eaten candy
knows how sweet candy is. Just as you can't express the
sweetness of candy—you can only say that it is sweet—you
cannot express the joy of your living existence when you
are generating energy by your own power.

Sa Ta Na Ma is the compound of a particular sound. 13
When you put your physical energy into creating a particular sound, what happens? The tongue is arranged to speak
it, the ears are told to hear it, the eyes close down to meditate on it, the outer self is forced to communicate at the
level of the inner self, and union will take place.

The highest gift a man can be given in his life is that he 14
hears the word from the tongue of a person who sincerely,
mentally, one-pointedly believes and practices it. Any communication which is beyond doubt is always very effective.
Word is not only what you speak, but also expression.
Through eyes, through ears, when you smell the fragrance
of a rose in a garden, what do you say? What is the line of
communication? How is it communicated to you? Who is
communicating to whom? Self is communicating to the inner self, your own self; the structured self is communicating
to the inner self and who is responding to the communication? Yourself. Then what is beyond yourself? Nothing.
Then why do you act crazy and angry at people? What can
they give you?

For anyone who will live up to his word to infinity, this 15
world will become too small. It will seem as small as a Ping-
Pong ball. The whole universe will dance on the word of
that man. This is the vibratory effect an individual has,
because your end is infinity. Your beginning is infinity. You
are only in trouble when you have not realized you are infinity. To realize the infinity in the finite state is the exten-
sion of the mind. That is the reality of the mind.

The blend of your soul, mind, and body makes you talk. 16
This is the art of vibration. If your mind is off you cannot talk
sensibly. If your soul is off you don't exist. Hence, it is a
blending of the three that makes you vibrate. You vibrate
anyway, but vibration in the form of communication is effectively recognized when you talk. Word was with God
and communicated with maya to create this universe and its
beauty. Word is with you. Communicate to create your
own world.

Man has to understand that he is a center of the universal 17
psyche because he is a part of the universal psyche. The
word is not beautiful without him; he is not beautiful without
word.

If you will meditate on the primal sound you will see the 18
unseen, you will hear the unheard, and you will feel the
unfeelable.

All you have to do in your whole life is to join with one   19
word through which you can feel that your finite personality
is joined with the infinite. That is all you need. Learn it
through any religion, any yoga master, through any swami,
through a butcher, through anybody. Learn it. It is imma-
terial from whom; but learn it. This is why they say, "That
mean, mean man whom nobody knows, when he medi-
tates on the Nam, the four corners of the world will bow to
him."

Word was with God, word will be with you. Cause will   20
lead to effect, sequence will lead to consequence.

Talking is not just talking. Talking is the mixture of the   21
trinity of the person and it is the vibratory effect of man. If
you remember that God sits on the tip of the tongue of
man, you will be very cautious about what you do with it.
The tongue is not an insignificant thing, although it lives
amidst thirty-two teeth. It is the most flexible part of the
body, the most sensitive part of the body, as well as the
most effective part of the body. A word said by the tongue
can cut through the heart in a way which no medicine can
cure. And sweetness from the tongue can bring you the
total wealth of the world.

Any word that you speak exists. It is there. It is a vibra-   22
tion. Word is a cause and an effect. Nobody can escape
from word. Realizing that we can't escape word is our basic
duty.

I know of a man, who used to say, "God bless you. May you be restored to health." His virtues were many. People with diseases which we cannot imagine would ever be cured used to get cured by his word. So I became very interested in studying that man. To my surprise he used to say one word whenever he talked and that word was *tuhi, tuhi, tuhi* — "thou, thou, thou." If you gave him food, he would say "thou, thou, thou"; water, "thou, thou, thou"; slap him, "thou, thou, thou." He went through every experience saying, "thou, thou, thou." When people requested him to go to a sick man's house, all he said was, "With thy grace be healthy, his mercy upon thee." It took one hour, two hours, three hours, and the man would get up. This is the power of vibration; you talk through the mind, not only through the tongue; when you talk through the tongue, there is a mind behind it, mental thoughts. We do not value these mental thoughts enough. If the mind vibrates with the mantra you chant, the effect will be tremendous, accurate, beautiful. When you say "Ek," the whole universe should look to you as Ek. When you say "Ong," the spring season and the seed sprout unfold in the universe. When you say "Kar," the moon, sun, stars, any beautiful thing ever lived by you in your mental thoughts should become a spotlight for you. When you say "Sat," you should feel illuminated. "Nam" should give you existence in your humility. "Siri," the miracle of this creation, should be acknowledged by you. And after that you should fall into the ecstasy by saying "Wha," and the total merge should happen when you say "Guru." If you take every care that verbalization is supported by the mind when you chant a mantra, I cannot describe what you can be.

God sits on the tip of the tongue of the holy man. When   24
the holy man speaks, God becomes a slave to his words.
Remember what John said: "In the beginning was the Word
and the Word was with God and the Word was God."

A man can be judged from the vibration he makes—the   25
language he speaks and the way he relates to other people.
You can pinpoint a person by the way he speaks one sen-
tence. You can know how divine that person is. If he
speaks a universal language he lives in a universal consciousness.

If your words have the strength of the infinite in them and   26
you value them and they are virtuous, you are the greatest
of the great. If you do not value your words, you have no
value. Your own word is your value as a human being.
Your word is your value. In the beginning was the Word
and the Word was with God and the Word was God.

A polluted mind deludes one's sense of self, and   27
sometimes the sense of self is so deluded that self-respect is
lost. When self-respect is lost, grace is lost; when grace is
lost, the word is lost; when the word is lost, then sacrifice is
lost. Sacrifice can only happen when you know the word. If
you give a promise, you must live up to it. If you commit,
you must live up to it. If you know something is a truth, you
must live it; and if you can't do that, what else can you do?

Everything must change, this is a law of the universe; but you will change either for your higher values or for your lower values. If you change for higher values, you will live for the word. If you live for lower values, you will betray your own word. 28

When you betray your own word, then you betray your own concept; and when you betray your own concept, then the entire universe will know nothing but to betray you. 29

Man has to understand within his own depth that within himself is the word which he has only to experience within himself. Without that, there is no *mukti,* liberation. A teacher can always give you technical know-how. He can teach you techniques, but not the experience. He will stand by, then the experience will happen. Be kind to him, love him, respect him, give him reverence, give him presents, whatever; I don't care what you do because you are doing it only to satisfy yourself. 30

Those who do not know how to live to their words shall never have the knowledge to know God. 31

Love

Understanding and humility lead to the perfection of love, 32
and God is love.

Male and female make a union and this complete union is 33
the greatest yoga.

Marriage is when there are two bodies and but one soul.

The moment you can love the being of an individual, then 34
you love the God of an individual; the moment that experience happens, then you become a universal soul yourself.

Love is the experience of sacrifice in one's self. 35

Why can't you love everybody? You have no tolerance. 36
You have to learn to hold your temper, you have to learn
not to slander, you have to learn to have patience, you
have to learn to be humble.

Love is a sacrifice. Love is not a projection; love is an attraction. 37

Love means giving. Self-sacrifice means that you accomplish for someone at the expense of yourself. 38

The purpose of the being is to receive love from the Unknown. 39

God means total creativity, but the power of love is beyond that. Why? Because all of creativity is the offering of love. Total existence is based on love. 40

The power of love is not positive and it is not negative. It is both positive and negative. 41

Man seeks inspiration, recognition, and confirmation of his personality in a polarity opposite to him which is woman. The fourth thing that he seeks is expansion—on a physical level, on a spiritual level, and on a mental level. On a physical level, it is the service we do for each other; on a mental level, it is the inspiration that we give to each other; on a spiritual level, it is the trust that we have in each other. If these three things are present, we develop confidence in each other. Then, the two people can experience a kind of love. 42

You don't want somebody to hate you; you want all to 43
love you. Actually, love is a hatred and hatred is a love;
there is no difference. In one, ego is satisfied; in one, ego is
not. When ego is not satisfied, it is a hatred; when ego is
satisfied, it is a love.

Love is to sacrifice and find the self within one's self. 44

Love is a self-sacrifice. Love is the experience within one's 45
self of one's own selflessness; that's why love is God. No
one can explain love, because love is ecstasy. Love is the
essence of an ever-longing devotion. Love does not
change. If love changes, it is not love.

When a man knows himself, he knows every self. When 46
a man loves himself, he loves every self.

Love is a sacrifice, love has no limit. When it has a limit, 47
then it is not love.

Sacrifice is the beginning of every love. One must subject 48
one's self in order to receive an object. How many of us can
subject ourselves?

Man cannot live without love, he must love and also he   49
must be loved. Love is the highest fulfillment on every level.
When you are recognized, it is an expression of love; when
a present is given to you, it is an expression of love; when
someone communicates to you, it is an expression of love;
when someone smiles at you, it is an expression of love. All
these are expressions of love. But can you be satisfied with
expressions? No, you want to experience something. Even
when you have physical or verbal or mental intercourse, are
you loved? No. These are also expressions of love. Then
what is love? When you feel and experience selflessness
within yourself and you can vibrate for someone, then you
are fulfilled with love. This is the highest state of individual
consciousness; everything else is beautiful. These feelings
are of such fulfilling beauty that we do not have the
vocabulary at our command to explain them, and our in-
ability to explain only tells us that these feelings exist like
ecstasies. If you can explain ecstasy, it is not an ecstasy.

The sexual union is actually and absolutely divine. It pro-   50
vides an experience that man can find in any experience,
that of God-consciousness. But a lot of brainwashing has
been done and man's practical living habits have deterior-
ated. Consider a young man in his twenties who meets a
young girl, and they fall in love. There is a very powerful
feeling that is called longing for each other. This instinct of
longing is the most powerful instinct, because it can prevent
the totality of the psyche of the universe from acting in relation and according to the individual psyche. This most
powerful unknown power of the individual can be realized
in one relationship only: the relationship between male and
female. There is no way you can understand the impact
and the depth of this relationship. We call it love in practice.

I'm not talking of love in imagination or love of people; I'm talking of love in action, when man feels for another individual. It is an attraction of polarities; one polarity seeks to merge with another to create a neutral state of mind. It is very unfortunate that in 1977 neither do men know how to do this nor do women know what it is.

In sexual love we have lost integrity. When we feel we are 51 hungry, we are supposed to eat; so when we feel passionate, we feel we are supposed to have sex. That's what sexual love has become today. When man loses the sense of reproductivity and the honor for his seed, man loses the value of self-respect. When you do not value the seed, what do you value? A farmer who does not care for the quality of his seed, nor for the quality of his land, does not care to preserve the seed, does not care to sow it in a proper line. Do you call him a good farmer?

Woman

Do one favor for yourself. Never be ungrateful in a rela- 52
tionship to any woman. For if you do not respect a symbol,
then you do not respect your clarity of consciousness, and
woman is a symbol of regeneration. We call it the symbol of
Adi Shakti.

Love and respect a woman voluntarily, with no compul- 53
sion. There should be knowledge, there should be awareness of each individual. This must be the first rule or there
shall never be peace, there shall be agony on the planet
Earth.

The one yoga of all yoga is married life; a deep under- 54
standing of a woman, a deep understanding of a man, a
deep understanding of human relationship, coordination,
togetherness, coziness of the self and the relationship.

First recognize the creativity of the Creator. The moment 55
a woman recognizes and understands that she is the creativity of the Creator, confidence as a woman comes to her.

You cannot love me if you will not love your first teacher, 56
who is woman. You are born of a woman. If you do not
learn to respect woman, the Supreme Consciousness will
not talk to you. You will end up with broken homes and
broken hearts.

When man tries to walk on the path of God, three things 57
will come to him in abundance: women, money, and land.
Why have I said women? The test of a male in his steadiness of consciousness is when he can prove his roots are
deep, and he who is born of woman is always tested by a
woman. Don't misunderstand me. Let me make it very
clear. The man who gives his word is always tested by a
woman.

By construction, the fulfillment of a woman is 58
motherhood; and motherhood does not mean that she gets
pregnant and delivers a baby. If you understand her total
behavior, you will understand her motherhood. Her
motherhood is service, her motherhood is sacrifice, her
motherhood is relationship. When she knows motherhood,
she is fulfilled. But when she becomes a partner with man
she shares equally.

A woman who is capable of giving birth must give birth to 59
a saint, a hero, or a giver.

Any woman on this planet who values herself as a 60
woman is great, and she is a giver of life; and when you are
a giver of life, what more can you do?

If you do not understand a woman, you cannot reach God, because you do not know how to get away from *maya*, illusion.   61

If the woman stops looking to the male for inspiration and stability, then the male has lost everything. It becomes a matter of existence, not a matter of relationship, because the side of the moon which shines looks toward the sun.   62

As a man you are born of a woman. When you grow, you want a woman. Eventually you marry with a woman and have children. Your A-to-Z structure is around and around a woman. You want to be rich for a woman, you want to be poor for a woman, you want to move to the country for a woman, you want to come to the city for a woman. Whether you admit it or deny it, basically you are a slave of woman in one way or another.   63

People who have the idea that a woman is a weak and frail creature do not know what a woman is. A woman is sixteen times stronger than a man.   64

The man who does not know the art of relaxing the female partner in any sexual cohabitation will never maintain the grounds of married life.   65

Happiness

The law of equilibrium is the law of happiness. Everything 66
can be sacrificed but equilibrium.

Happiness is carefreeness in consciousness. 67

Without realizing who you are, happiness cannot come 68
to you.

The core of unhappiness lies when the self does not 69
recognize the self; and the core of happiness is when the
self recognizes the self.

Dear ones, never blame anyone or anything. Whatever 70
happens, you must have asked for it, and you must have
asked for it for a purpose. Have patience, for patience pays.

The greatest tragedy is that everybody says that he can 71
give you the secret to happiness. This is the biggest lie on
this planet. Nobody can give anybody happiness; it is im-
possible. And we are so eager to buy happiness that when
someone says he can give happiness, we all fall for it.

Why do people worship God? For happiness. Why do people get married? For happiness. Why do people divorce? For happiness. Everything is done in the name of and for happiness. Still there is no happiness. What makes a man unhappy? When he has a desire and it is not satisfied. It does not matter what the desire is. **72**

Each experience must lead to your happiness and grace. **73**

Man suffers for one reason: Man loses his innocence. When you lose your innocence, you end up with dispute. To regain innocence so that universal consciousness will serve and maintain you is the idea of this yoga. **74**

If you can remember that you are a part of infinity, then no wrong can happen to you. **75**

There is no way to define God but as a totality. When you know your totality, you will not have fear. You must be righteous; when you are righteous, you are effective. When you are effective, you are magnetic. When you are magnetic, the sun's energy gives you polarity; then you must be neutral. When you are neutral, then you are God-conscious. When you are God-conscious you are in harmony with the universe and the universe is in harmony with you. Total creativity relates to you as a nuclear center of a psychomagnetic field; then you are in an absolute state of bliss. **76**

Happiness comes out of contentment, and contentment   77
always comes out of service.

Who is unhappy? One who has nothing to flow with and   78
one who has too much to know what to do with that flow.

All sickness, all shallowness, all unhappiness, all pain, all   79
miseries are the outcome of one source; keeping negativity
within yourself.

Who am I and what do I know? These are questions that   80
man has to ask himself. He must realize the unknown of
him and become the total known self. This is destiny.

Awareness is the total sum of the individual's ac-   81
knowledgment of the universal existence around him.
Anyone who is very much extended in that sphere will find
a greater happiness in his relationship to the infinity around
him.

Happiness comes from contentment. If you make a sur-   82
vey of how many people are happy and unhappy, you will
be surprised in this life sketch that what you feel as happiness, another man will see as sickness. So never judge
anybody's happiness by your standards.

There was a man of God living on a hill, in a little hut with few disciples. He was content. A king went before him and offered a lot of gold pieces. The king said, "Oh, man of God, I want in my life to serve somebody. I want to give this to you." The man of God looked at him and said, "Thank you very much, now carry it back." This annoyed the king, who said, "What are you talking about? I brought this all the way up here by myself and you do not even care for it. Why won't you accept it?" The man of God replied, "I don't want to be murdered tomorrow so better take it away. You perhaps don't want to live. This gold was meant for those places where there are guards. Here God lives, not guards. You better leave along with the gold." Now who doesn't want gold? But it's like that; if you have gold you must have guards. If you have the guards you will have their problems. If you have this, you must have that, and on and on. 83

Life is a game, but we do not want to play unattached. We want to play for the sake of winning and losing, and that is where unhappiness comes in. 84

Where is the limit of a person? How can you be limited? A person is limited according to his attachment. It doesn't matter what you have or what you don't have; it matters only how easily you can let go. 85

The mind should dance with the body, and the whole universe is your stage. Try to feel that whatever you are doing is the most beautiful thing, the prettiest dance, because you are dancing with the whole universe. Don't resent anything. Let your heart guide you, free of all regimentation. 86

Flexibility is a law of life. In our common language we call 87
it compassion.

If any person is unhappy, it is because he wished for 88
unhappiness. When you wish for happiness, you also wish
indirectly for unhappiness, just as day precedes night and
night precedes day. Every happiness is followed by sadness
and every sadness is followed by happiness.

The moment you feel that you are a part of infinity and 89
that infinity is a part of you, your limitations will cease and
happiness will flow.

Living on this earth does not matter if we have lived with 90
grace, and fundamentally we know that living on this earth
with grace is all that matters. If we have not lived on this
earth gracefully, it will be very difficult to leave this earth
gracefully.

It is very important to realize that happiness lies within us. 91
The amount of happiness that lies within us depends on
how open, how positive, and how accurately righteous we
are. This is the secret of happiness.

Why do we tell you to remember God? What is there that 92
you should remember or not remember? What are you going to gain? The moment a man realizes that potentially he
is infinite and he is only limited in activity, he can be happy.
If something goes wrong, he should not give in. He knows
that he can regenerate, recapture, and redo. If God is with
you, then you are great. You can take it.

When your doubts are gone, then your fears will be 93
gone. Your feelings and experiences will be of happiness.

It is God who created you and it is to God that you will go. 94
Nothing exists in between. This world is a temporary visita-
tion. Visit it with love and remember that if you have not
learned to leave this earth in happiness, your soul shall be
stuck on this earth.

In this world, if we can only learn to respect the concern of 95
others, then we can have happiness.

Self

W hat is meditation? What is God-consciousness? What is   96
truth? What are you seeking? If you think very deeply, very
consciously, the answer will come to you. You are a living
existence of light; you need not seek anything.

P atience pays. Let no temptation shake you, no vibration   97
move you, and no action force you out of yourself and righteousness. An unshakable human being is the highest living
phenomenon of God.

Y ou are you and you are nothing else but you; but when   98
it comes to testing you, you immediately fail if you don't
know you are you.

T he purpose of knowledge is to develop infinite faith in   99
self.

W hen a man becomes God-conscious, he becomes hum-   100
ble enough to present his entire personality before the world
without fear.

Nothing on earth can divide you from your real self. Re- 101
late to this life creatively. All the pain and pleasure that you
experience is your personal story.

The whole world is to realize yourself what you are and to 102
be what you are. Do not inflate and do not deflate. Find the
median point. The problem with man is that he is asked,
"Are you this or are you that?" But you are not this nor that,
you are as you are.

To recognize the truth, first recognize that you are the 103
truth.

If you are not aware for you and aware of you, then your 104
existence will be damaged. If you want to be great, then
you will have to feel great and act great. Many people think
they have to seek approval. All you have to do is approve
of yourself.

If you are not aware of someone else, then in reality you 105
are not aware of yourself.

The moment you meet a man of God-consciousness, he 106
will tell you, "Know thyself."

If you achieve righteousness throughout your life and con- 107
versation, it doesn't matter who you are or to whom you
belong. The goal is achieved.

Man is like a candle: He must radiate light by burning   108
himself.

You don't have to realize God and you don't have to real-   109
ize infinity; all you have to do is realize your existence.

The inner self of the self is sitting, waiting for you to realize   110
that self.

Once you are known as a straightforward and outspoken   111
person, that's it. There cannot be any difficulty. When you
twist things, not only do you waste your energy in twisting,
actually you twist your own image. Remember that there is
no such thing as a secret. The cat will always come out of
the bag, and you will feel bad about it. Why? Your own
consciousness will hurt you.

Liberation is from the subconscious mind, the watchdog   112
of the self, the recorder of the self.

A man has to understand his existence in relationship to   113
the universe. Whosoever knows this knows the truth. The
whole world around you will be beautiful if you understand
that you are you.

Universal realization comes when you see yourself as   114
nothing but a *bindu*, a point. What is *tantra*? Tantra is the
science of the point.

Kindness, forgiveness, and righteousness are the tripod 115
on which rests the God-consciousness of the being.

No one wants to become limited, because each one is in- 116
finite; the source of you is infinity.

Nobody should meditate and chant except for realization 117
of self. Your self is very precious. If you want to experience
the infinite consciousness, which is God, you can only experience that through the self.

Your very existence is truth; surrender to it. You will be 118
grateful.

Our realization is through our own soul; the very realiza- 119
tion of the self within the structured self is the greatest
achievement.

You are the effect of a cause and there is a creator in you. 120

The basic unit, you, is equal to radiance plus activity. 121

When you become light and you radiate, there is no 122
darkness. A candle has one future, to spread the light. How
does the candle spread the light? By burning itself, the candle spreads light and consequently knows the future. If you
burn yourself, you will radiate and will spread light. The job
of the human being is to radiate through the finite self the
infinite light.

Be creative, be loving, be giving, be great, and God will give you bounty. There will be no limit. Whatever you plant in the spring, it will grow. So, if in your own ecology you will sprout positivity, service, smiles, charm, happiness, good faith, you will grow and you will be unlimited. 123

If you don't have self-reliance, what do you have? You can cross the mountains, the oceans, the tragedies, the difficulties, the responsibilities, with only one thing, self-reliance. Fear not, my dear ones; the antidote for fear is self-reliance. 124

A person of self-realization is also a man of gracefulness, a man of his word, and powerfully forgiving. These are the four qualities of a yogi. 125

Why do we cling to the past? Because we are insecure. We are insecure about our self-realization, and therefore, we do not have self-confidence. 126

I am nonviolent, but if I see that the weak is being molested by the unrighteous, I will be first to put myself between the two. It may cost me my life but to me it is worth it. That is the grace of the inner being. And when you put your life as an offering on the altar of truth, that is the highest sacrifice. 127

If thou knowest that Thou is in thee, then why do you ask, who is He? 128

If a deer has a wonderful smell of musk in his navel, he gets   129
the aroma and he runs and runs and runs to find from
where the aroma is coming. Sometimes he runs to the
north, sometimes he runs to the south. He runs, and then
in his running he gets stuck, and his neck bends back into
his navel when he falls; and when he gets his nose into his
navel, he then knows that the aroma was in his navel all
along. At that moment he wonders why he was running so
hard for the beauty, but he never realized that the fragrance
that was so enchanting, the beauty that he was trying so
desperately to find was nowhere else but in his very navel.
Just so, the soul that rivals God is in us, and we should
recognize it.

Man is basically unlimited because the soul is unlimited.   130
Man is basically unlimited because his mind is unlimited.
Only the physical structure is limited, but the structure is
priceless. Nobody can manufacture it.

A man of God should develop a reliance on truth, on self,   131
on higher self, on wisdom, on spirit, on mind, on physical
abilities and capacities. And a man of God should develop
and guide this reliance so that when he walks out and faces
the world, he is wise.

You are what you relate to. If you relate to an infinity, you   132
are an infinity. But if you limit yourself, then you are
limited.

There are ways to feel relaxed. One is to feel that you are 133
a part of the universe and that the universe is a part of you.
You are just as beautiful as the universe. Without you, the
universe is not beautiful, and you are not beautiful without
the universe.

The moment you become aware of who you are, 134
everyone on this planet will become aware of who you are.
Your only setback is when you are not aware of who you
are. You are not only one thing, but you are everything all
the time, under all circumstances.

You must understand that you are three selves. One is 135
your body, with its desires. One is your mind, with its
thoughts. And one is you, with your controlling whip. Most
people do not know that the mind and the self are two
separate things. The mental self and the higher self are two
separate things. If you cannot recognize the fight in you between these three selves, then you know absolutely
nothing. But gradually you will realize this conflict within
you, and you will be able to overcome that conflict so that
the higher self may win.

And anyone who values himself egolessly is a living God. 136

Actually, the person who has realized God is very hum- 137
ble. A man who has seen millions of dollars and tons of
jewelry is not going to snatch your watch. The man who
feels the Creator of this creation will be in such ecstasy that
he achieves humility.

If you want to know the Infinite, know the finite first: Know 138 thyself.

You have to be you, but you can only be you when you 139 understand that you are a part of infinity. The moment that you understand you are a part of infinity, then you become a living God.

Never forget that you are a *bindu,* a pinpoint. 140

Life is an attitude. You have to basically decide, once and 141 for all, whether you are going to be original or not.

Your potential self is unlimited; your active self is limited. 142

The following six characteristics—the way a man behaves, 143 the way a man worships, the way a man imagines, the way a man dresses, the way a man deals, and the way a man addresses people—all these things determine what the man is.

You are a human being. "Hue" means light, the aura; 144 "man" means mind; "being" means the now. Now you are the mental light.

Self-relaxation is the highest discipline. A relaxed man 145 can communicate with man. An unrelaxed man cannot communicate with man. An unrelaxed man cannot communicate with God, Who is the total sum of all humanity.

There is a reason we are here and that reason is to remain   146
graceful and face all ungraceful environments with grace.
This is the purpose and it is a privilege.

We have to understand within ourselves that if the inner   147
self is secure, our outside is secure, happy, calm, cozy,
beautiful, whatever you want to call it. If the inner self is disturbed, our outer self is disturbed and we see the whole
world around us as disturbed.

Whether my mind relates to it or not, I am not mind.   148
Whether my body relates to it or not, I am not body. I am
that which is beyond body and beyond mind—Wha.

In our human body and in our consciousness there is no   149
higher value than to become a seeker.

In the self is a universe and it is a miniform of the universe.   150
One who will not understand the microconsciousness will
never understand the macroconsciousness.

Not only do you have the potential to do everything, but   151
you must recognize that potential.

Worship your own self, your own glory, your own power   152
of sacrifice and service.

You must remember one thing: When you have knowl-   153
edge, you will not have fear.

The power of the individual lies in the fact that the entire universe rotates around him. 154

Without labor one never understands the master within himself. 155

One thing you cannot copy and that is the soul of another person or the spirit of another person. It is the spirit in you that matters. 156

Meditation is a duty toward the self. The moment you become aware of the self, you become beautiful to self because the moment you concentrate on self, your frequency changes and the universe around you changes also. This is a cosmic law. 157

There is nothing more precious than the self. There is nothing more beautiful than the self. There is nothing greater than the self. Only with the self can you realize that there is a God, a Supreme Consciousness of the Supreme Self. 158

What is man's destiny? Man's destiny is to merge with infinity. You should not only know it, you should experience it. Experiencing in yourself the vastness of infinity is the aim of human life. 159

Whether you believe me or not, there is a chance for 160
every man to become a perfect saint. If your mental attitude
is perfect and security and calmness is achieved inside,
everything, all the material world, will relate to you outside.

The greatest education man has to learn is not medical 161
science, not sociology, not chemistry, not biology, not
mathematics, but the science of man, the science of self.
The science of self and self-awareness is the highest knowledge a man can possess because then you can pull through
all circumstances.

You are all denying the basic values because for two thou- 162
sand years man has been told that he is a sinner and that he
has to redeem himself. Actually, a man is born in absolute
love and grace. He is born in total fulfillment of his joy and
happiness. This is the real truth, but holy men who lived on
the money of householders have created such a fear complex that they have frightened many people. A difference
that has to be understood by any man is that God is not outside, that God is not anywhere. God starts as charity starts,
right from one's own home.

If you are told to meditate in individuality to universality, it 163
only means to recognize your own value, your own merit,
consciously; and if you can only do this, then everything
will be all right.

Wisdom

T hose who know the law is to be together; then everything   164
will come together for them.

 I f you want to refrain from something, refrain when you   165
are young. Youth is the time of life when you can do anything. It is during the time of old age that the bloody wolf
declares, "Now I have become a vegetarian," because after
losing his teeth he can't hunt anything.

 I t doesn't matter who you are. All that matters is that when   166
the clouds strike you, you can pull yourself up. That is all
that matters.

 I f you want the delicacy of life, if you want the delicacy of   167
living, then you have to live as a guest. Come, enjoy, and
leave with grace.

 W hen thou shalt hear the truth with the center of the two   168
eyes, the third eye, thou shalt never forget it.

One is wise and one is foolish. Everybody has some   169
wisdom and some foolishness. It is a mixture. There is only
a difference in percentage, not in totality.

A wise man, a spiritual man, is that man who is neutral in   170
a relationship.

Your deeds shall decide whether God is near to you or   171
away from you.

What you are you are, and destiny is destiny. Make a dog   172
emperor and still he will lick the grinding wheel.

When there is a time to stay, one should stay. When   173
there is a time to go, one should go. When there is a time to
fight, one should fight. When there is a time to have, one
should have; but it should all be graceful.

Your deeds should be honorable as you want to be   174
received by God. And your deeds cannot be honorable unless you have honorable intentions. If you want to kill
someone, first you must kill your own feelings. If you want
to take from someone, first take away your own pride.

Whatever you are, you are. Be proud of it.   175

Those who learn to live on the primal vibration of God,   176
they are the bright-faced, they are the light of light, and
their job is done.

When you start loving God, he starts putting money into 177
your life or a lovely woman or a temptation like power or
authority. He puts it before you to see if you will let it go, to
see who you love most.

The mystery is—do you know that the great unknown 178
One is you?

One who speaks the truth shall go, but the truth he 179
speaks shall not go.

Have you ever thought of it, that sometimes, in spite of 180
your best effort and will, you are unable to do a particular
thing? And sometimes with the best effort to deny a situation, you get into it?

The mind is like a mirror through which you can see infin- 181
ity. But if you put the blackness of hatred over it, you will
see nothing.

There is much wisdom around us but there is no heart to 182
feel it, there is no brain to compute it, and there is no compassion to understand it.

Everybody has been kind enough to leave this planet and 183
we must leave it, so why bother about it? Where is the problem? If you have no problem coming, why create a problem
going? As you come in innocence, go in innocence, and
don't worry.

Truth does not need introduction. When the sun rises, is 184
there necessity to announce it?

When spring comes, nature sprouts, blooms, talks to 185
you. Roses are there with their fragrance to reach you.
Flowers open up their hearts to tell you how to open up
your heart.

After I had studied with a teacher for some time, he asked 186
me, "What have you learned?" So we sat down and we
talked and we shared food and he asked me again, "What
have you learned?" And I replied to him, "I am not this, I
am not that, I have seen the demonstration of it." He said,
"You have seen it, you have preserved it, you have
observed it, you have felt it, but has your mind changed
with that frequency?" I said, "No, it will take a little time."
Then he said, "So long as you can measure time, you are
not God-conscious." I don't know whether at that time he
was God or not but the experience totally opened my third
eye. "All right," I said to him, "I am at your feet. You have
taught me the essence of Godhead in projective mind and
consciousness." He then restated the truth. He said, "At
your command, if mind—which is above time—has to be
measured by time by you, that is the difference between
God and you."

The strength of the man does not lie in what he has. The 187
strength of the man lies only in what he can give. Only
those can give who have the capacity to tap into the
universe. If the universe is not in your mind, your heart cannot give.

Advise only those whom your advice suits. Never advise 188 a monkey, he will mess up your house. Never give advice to anybody if you don't want enemies.

There is no doubt that we are all very wise. If anybody 189 doubts that he is wise, he is only doubting the exercise of that wisdom, not the wisdom itself.

There is no such thing as an accident. It is all part of a 190 master plan. Play your role as gracefully as you can and relax.

Wisdom becomes knowledge when it becomes your per- 191 sonal experience.

Why are we limited? Because of lack of wisdom through 192 knowledge. If you know wisdom and then you go through an experience, you have knowledge. Then you are one step higher and one step higher and one step higher. Any wisdom which you experience within yourself becomes a knowledge within you. A man of wisdom will fall. A man of knowledge will never fall.

We can understand how easy life can be if we can just be 193 as we are.

If you want to rule the world, there is only one law: the law 194 of compassion and the sweet tongue.

What use is a flower with no fragrance? What use is a mir-   195
ror in which you cannot see yourself? You must know your
soul and project it.

Feel good, do good, and be good. These are the only   196
goods you can carry along with you; all the rest belongs to
the planet Earth.

Life is an unsolved mystery. Those who solve it don't talk   197
about it. Those who don't solve it talk a lot.

A life with contentment is the life of an emperor. A life of   198
moderate desires is the life of a king. And a life of impatient
desires is the life of a beggar.

In spite of your best efforts, with all the medical science at   199
your command, with your ego and your desires, you are to
leave one day.

What is yesterday is gone; what is today is tomorrow;   200
because every step we take today shall reflect our tomorrow. Worry not whether you will go to heaven or to hell. It
is the will of the Creator who created heaven and hell
together.

During the first three years, a mother gives the child what   201
it needs. Then for eight years the child relates to the image
of the father. From twelve years to eighteen, in the case of a

woman, or to twenty years in the case of a man, it is the relatives and the environment that guide the person; and after that it is the spiritual teacher of the consciousness within the self that guides the person. This is how a person moves in the orbit of life.

A man was traveling in a car and he saw somebody 202 traveling on a horse. He said, "Ha, ha, look at him. What is he doing?" The man who was going on a horse saw some-one who was going on a donkey, and he said, "Look at this fellow, he is really poor." The man who was going on a donkey also saw someone who was going on foot, and he said, "Look at that poor fellow, he has to walk all day." The man who was walking saw another man with a broken leg, and he said, "Oh, it is a tragedy." We speculate because we have never found ourselves. Contentment comes to those who have found their center. Great are those beings who have found the Being of beings.

Time is now; now is the time. 203

As for health, you need a doctor; as for school, you need 204 a teacher; as for your soul, you need a guide.

You have to understand the purpose of life. The purpose 205 of life is to do something which will live forever.

You never sin against somebody, you sin against yourself. 206

Fools live in fear, a wise man lives in strength. 207

You are very powerful provided you know how powerful 208
you are.

There is no student and there is no teacher, because there 209
is no child and there is no father.

Man knows what reality is, but he doesn't want to live it. 210

It is your unity that will exalt the God and the strength in 211
you, and it is your subjection to infinity that will make you
free.

If you want to keep lots of friends, never speak the truth. 212

What is it that people love most, but cannot have? A sage 213
answered, "Truth." Why? Because truth is nothing but a
universal mirror in which you can see yourself.

When one exalts the infinite, the infinite exalts that one; 214
when one exalts his teacher, then he himself will be exalted.

Wherever one bows, there he will be blessed. 215

If you want to learn a thing, read that; if you want to know 216
a thing, write that; if you want to master a thing, teach that.

The highest man is he who can uninvolve in every in- 217
volvement.

Without a giver there cannot be a taker; without a taker 218
there cannot be a giver.

Do not seek approval from others; seek approval from 219
yourself.

Everyone wants to know the truth, but nobody wants to 220
face it.

A graceful person is one who remains graceful even 221
through all ungraceful times. A happy person is one who
remains happy through all unhappy times.

Sometimes in our own emotions we try to guide the lives 222
of others. Wherever there is a devotion or love with somebody, you should make that one strong so that he can guide
his own life.

If you really want respect in this life, never advise anybody 223
without being asked; and secondly, when somebody really
asks you for advice, just wait until he is ready to listen; and
when you find the person is really ready to listen, then always give him polarity, the two sides of the subject as you
know it.

Preserve yourself. That is an art. It is an art to preserve   224
yourself. It is an art to selflessly serve somebody. It is an art
to give your total everlasting friendship. It is an art to understand all activity so caused by you in good faith, because
you are a living being. It is an art of gratitude. The attitude
of gratitude is the highest living experience in a human life. I
don't care whether you believe in Jesus or not, whether you
believe in God or not, whether you believe in Buddha or
not. This is not my problem, it is your problem. But be
grateful for every moment, for you must remember this moment will never come back.

Host those who have been your enemies, respect those   225
who have slandered you, and communicate with those who
have been all your life angry with you.

What is a sin? Betrayal of your own consciousness. A   226
Hindu takes meat, it is a sin from which he cannot be redeemed. A Muslim takes pork, it is a sin from which he cannot be redeemed. If a Christian doesn't take both, it is a sin
from which he cannot be redeemed.

When you cannot see the orange tree in the seed, how   227
can you see God in this world?

Don't deny the concept of infinite or finite. When you will   228
not deny, you will realize.

To be is not to be and not to be is Thee. When this secret is   229
known, the secret of self and universal self is known.

What is faith? Faith is what you believe. Who believes? 230
You. Who are you? Self. What is self? From where does it
come? Where is it going? These are very fundamental questions.

All colors are inside you. The universe is colorless. All 231
happiness is inside you. The universe is without happiness.
All sorrows are inside you. The universe is sorrowless. All
existence is inside you. The universe is existenceless.

If God asked the saints, "Why didn't you commit sins? 232
Why didn't you?" They would say, "Well, God, we loved
you." He would say, "Did you not know that I am merci-
ful?"

The great monk man said, "Know not. There is nothing in 233
the known."

When there is an end to a search, you have found. So 234
long as there is a search, you are searching. Where to end
the search, that is the question. End the search where you
meet a man of faith. Who is a man of faith? Talk to him on
any facet; if through every talk he shows you the path of
God, you have found him.

You know that without giving you don't take anything. 235
You know that without submitting yourself you will never
be exalted. You know that if you do not take deep roots
you will never flourish.

Everything is something and something is everything.　236

When you cannot sacrifice, you cannot give; and when　237
you cannot give, you cannot take; and that is the realm of
misery.

Silence is the most powerful speech; but there is an art to　238
be silent, and there is an art to speak.

Giving is a principle and it is an everlasting principle.　239
Your Creator gave you life, thus he became a giver.

It is not obligatory on the part of the wise man to give wis-　240
dom; it is obligatory for the man to ask the wise man for
wisdom.

If you will slander others, you will be slandered. If you will　241
love others, you will be loved. If you deceive others, you
will be deceived. If you give to others, you will be given to
by others.

Sobriety leads to purity. Purity leads to piety. Piety leads　242
to divinity. Divinity leads to universality; and that leads to
bliss, *ananda,* or whatever you want to call it.

To know wisdom is nothing. To experience wisdom be-　243
comes knowledge. Then you can stand through the times.

If there is happiness there is going to be sadness. If there is 244
sadness there is going to be happiness. Sadness attracts
happiness, happiness attracts sadness. This is the cycle.
Night is followed by day, clouds are followed by sunshine,
youth is followed by old age.

One who will claim will always blame. 245

God

From morning to evening we want you to meditate on one   246
thought: There is one Creator who created this universe.
He is truth personified. This is the mantra we chant.

A true seeker is one who will seek God in his heart.   247

God looks in people's hearts; he is the author of all   248
languages.

If you want to relate to the unseen, all you have to do is sit   249
down in a very easy and common position and *imagine,*
image in, that you are reaching Him. Don't think you are
performing a miracle; this is an easy thing.

What is God? Is He six hands? Ten heads? Is He a mat-   250
ter? Is He a body? No, He is cosmic energy; it prevails
through everybody. All that we can feel, can know, or can
imagine is God. His identity is Nam because He is Truth;
that is why we call Him Sat Nam. He is yin-yang; He is
positive and negative. He is male, female. He is the Creator
and his creation. That is why we say Sat Nam.

One day I asked somebody, "How many years have you 251
been trying to learn the spiritual way?" He said, "Thirty
years." I said, "In thirty years what you have learned?" He
said, "I just want to be, just to feel God. I just want to learn
to pay off my karma. I am not perfect. I am not complete. I
am not yet unattached." He asked five, six, seven questions. I said, "All you have to learn is to unlearn all of what
you have said, that's all you have to learn." He said, "How
can you say that to me?" I said, "Who made you? Who
constructed you? Who gave you this mind? Who gave you
this existence?" He said, "The cosmos. Some people call
Him God, also." I said, "Well, are you aware of that?" He
said, "Yes." I said, "Well, why don't you rely on it? Why
don't you read on the dollar bill, 'In God we trust' and rid
yourself of the whole problem?" Trust, *trust* itself is self-
realization. *I am, I am, is a self-trust,* and when this idea is
perceived, nothing else is required.

God wants his children to merge in Him. But the con- 252
sciousness is not equal to and cannot merge into that Supreme Consciousness. That is why the cycle of birth and
death continues.

The secret of knowledge is to talk about *the God* and not 253
about *your God.* If you will talk about *the God* and not *your
God* the whole world will be with you.

The wrath of God will come upon one who slanders other 254
people, because God gets annoyed when his creation is being slandered by his very creation.

Why are you afraid that God will not forgive you? His 255
name is forgiveness. So do not worry all the time or the fire
of worry will make a barbecue out of you.

Every creator loves his creation. A musician loves his   256
music, an artist loves his art, a chef loves his food. So God
loves his creation, and He created every creator with all his
totality.

A knot tied by the man of God cannot be untied by God,   257
but a knot given by God can be opened by a man of God.
Why? Because God reveals himself through his avatars,
through his devotees, through his love in the human body,
because the human body is the channel of creativity as a
creature of the Creator.

The totality in reality is creating, organizing, and destroy-   258
ing. This force, which is in constant action, is what God is.

When you say cosmic consciousness, you mean God.   259
When you say universal mind, you mean God. There is no
difference, there is just the difference in expression.

Let us meditate on God. By God, I mean the Infinite   260
Creator, the giver of energy, and the power through which
our breath fluctuates in us as we inhale and exhale; that
great Existence, that great Phenomenon of Truth in us
which brings us the satya and gives us the life. Unknown we
are, to Known we have to go. From the God who made the
blueprint of the being—the eyes, the nose, the hair, the
shoulders, the hands and arms—fill all of that with humility.
Draw from the universe that great energy and feel it in
every cell of your body. Let every cell of your body vibrate
and extend that vibration to every extent. Feel it as a big
whirlwind of energy circling with each cell of your body.
Just concentrate and feel it in you.

There is only righteousness; God is within. Don't think of   261
him on the third story. You are God; without Him you do
not exist.

God does not have time to punish everybody for wrong   262
actions. The very wrong action is a punishment in itself.
Please don't blame God. All He did was create you and
give you life energy. He lets you go free; go, man, do
whatever you want. Come back to me after sixty-four years
and four days. If you do all right, I'll see you; if not, well,
God bless you. Self-destruction—doing weird things all the
time, self-condemnation—condemning yourself all the
time, these actions have no other meaning than that you
have not valued the grace of God, the creative principle, for
your creation. You will create your own time by your own
acts.

What is Godhood? When you cannot find your length   263
and breadth, your height and depth, that is Godhood.

There is a concept in our lives of sin that God is going to   264
judge you on the last day. There is no such thing. You are
judged by your own conception, your own consciousness,
all the time. You are bothered every minute. That is
enough. It is a pretty heavy hell in which to live.

It is not everybody's karma to learn everything. If all   265
reached Godhood, then what would happen to the creation? God would be perturbed. God loves everybody. He is
not in a hurry. He has no jealousy, no ego, no involvement.
He has created this whole universe, given the body, let all
enjoy. God is not in a hurry for you all to have salvation, for

all to come and hug Him. He knows where you are and what you are doing. Whether you do it in private or in public, it is one and the same thing to Him. The Unknown knows everything. He is the secret eye of the self and it is in every self.

Everybody should be a giver because that is a God quality. Everybody should be a worker; that is a God quality. And everybody should be everybody; that is a God quality. 266

It is easy to be God because you have all the power. But it is more difficult to be a guru because you have no power of a god. When you direct a person in the right consciousness, it becomes the direct clash of the ego with another person. 267

Most of us do not know what God is and sometimes for fun's sake we do not believe in God. God does not send a letter to you saying, "Please recognize me." Never. None of you has received a Christmas card from Him. God doesn't exist because of you at all, you exist because of Him, or It. A human being is a creature, a puppet hung on the string of breath. And you do not have control of your own breath. When you do not breathe, you do not breathe. Nothing on this planet is known to you which can make you breathe; nothing; understand that fundamentally. 268

God has as many elements as you can imagine in his infinite capacity. 269

Man has to live in his practical reality and truth, because Truth is God and God is Truth. 270

God is not a phenomenon. He is infinite. He is infinite, 271
but God is finite also. He is also a human being Who talks,
Who shakes hands with you, Who dances with you. He
does everything with you. We must understand this energy,
that the Infinite is also finite. Why are your arms in your
shoulders? Why not in the hips? Why do you have two
eyes, why not one big eye in the center? Why don't you
breathe through the knees? Why do you have a nose in the
center of your head? There is an architect who has made
you a blueprint. You have been constructed according to
this blueprint design and figure; that energy, beyond all expectations, cannot be denied.

If a man has grace in his personality, it is evidence that God 272
has found him. Contentment only means that man has an
attitude of gratitude while alive.

God is not living on the seventh story and no lift goes to 273
him. God is you, He is your expression. He is your identity
in existence. That is why God is everywhere. Because
wherever you are, God is. Because wherever you generate,
organize, and destroy, it is a fraction of the same that is
already prevailing in universal man. Therefore, we can con-
clude that man is the image, or the finite activity, of the
universal activity in operation.

It is true that between man and God there is no difference. 274
The difference is in the realization. Man has never realized
that he is God, man has always realized that he is man. He
is a human being. As a human being he has never realized
that there is a being inside him. In him there is an infinite being.

We have not realized in ourselves our own originality. 275
We have not realized in ourselves our total potency. We
always relate to our limitedness. O mind, you are a light
and you are a living light, but know who you are. Who am
I? Am I a finger? Yes, I am a finger, for action; but I am not
a finger. Am I a brain? Yes, for action I am a brain, but I am
not a brain. Am I a heart? Yes, for action I am a heart, but I
am not a heart. Then what am I? I am a combination of a
functional activity. If I am a combination of a functional activity, what is my source? My source is beyond me. And
what is my beyond point? Infinity. Call it God, call it Buddha, call it anything.

God is not what you say. God is a realization. Word is a 276
communication.

We have never realized what God is. On the other hand, 277
we say, "God is omnipresent, omniscient, and omnipotent." We say it. We know it. We all agree to it. We expect
to find Him in a church, in a temple; we find Him here, we
find Him there. God is a stick, God is a cup, God is a man,
God is a woman; God is everything and God is nothing—
everything which exists in any totality. A molecule has an
atom, an atom has an electron, proton, neutron, and the
permutation and combination of electron, neutron, and
proton are constant. That dance goes on, that vibration exists. Hindus call it *anhat*, Christians call it communion, Bud-
dhists call it light, Confucians call it wisdom. A Sikh knows it
as ecstasy. All is one and one is all.

The time has come when we should live as one. Forget 278
finding God, I do not know who God is. Let us be very
clean and honest and clear, and he will find us. Don't run
after him; he will run after you provided you know how to
stay clear, provided you know love, provided you know
how to stand honest.

Why did God create this world? Just to be recognized. It 279
is his instinct, and the same instinct is in us. We want to be
recognized as He wants to be recognized. We are the little
image of God, we are little Gods because we have a pineal
gland. The best way to be recognized is when your pituitary
starts working; then you know past, present, and future;
then you don't care; then you know what is what.

Whatever He is, He is you and you are He. 280

Don't worry. Only fools worry. Men of God always listen 281
to the song of God. If your body as one unit will praise God,
the whole world will praise you.

When you are happy, take it as a blessing of God. When 282
you are unhappy, take it as a test of God.

All teachings, whether they were taught in the past or 283
whether they are taught now or whether they will be taught
in the coming generations, have one idea alone, and the
only idea is to make a man realize God consciously. The
secret of all teachings, all masters, all gurus, all messengers,
all messiahs, is one—that at any stage, under any circumstances, man has the power to convert himself into a

superhuman being by consciously realizing the supreme God. We call it Godhead.

What is God-consciousness? God-consciousness is the totality in the human being. 284

Lord, you are the answer of every problem and you are the problem of every answer. 285

If God knows you can relax, He will love you. 286

There are many forms of meditation. There are forms of one meditation. There are many religions to know the origin, but actually there is one origin. There are many beings, part of the One Supreme Being. There are many truths of the Supreme Truth, but actually there is one Truth. There are many ways of the One Way; in reality there is only One Way. 287

Man can make God change; God cannot make man change. This is a cosmic law. The key can open the lock, the lock cannot open the key. The switch can turn on the night-light. 288

What does God mean in reality? It means the principle of generating, the principle of organizing, and the principle of destroying. It means the totality to create, the totality to run in, and the totality to destroy. That total totality means symbolically one word, God. Generation, organization, destruction—all equal God. 289

God is nothing but universality in experience. When you   290
experience a universal consciousness in your finite consciousness, that is what God is all about. When you say, "In
God we trust," it means, we trust in our own universal consciousness.

Reality only the Real One knows, and the Real One is the   291
One Who knows all the reality.

The one who has a Guru as a guide, and a God through   292
the Guru, has God and the Guru with him and he shall
never be alone.

God just sent you to earth as parents send their child to   293
kindergarten, to school, hoping that you will find some wisdom.

To deny a man and to sit in judgment on a human being is   294
to sit in judgment on God, because the Creator is responsible for the creature.

Eyes are the light of the soul, ears are the instrument of   295
the Divine, the tongue is the creativity of the Creator. This is
the Trinity which makes the totality of God-consciousness.

You know what a magician God is? He is the biggest trick   296
master I have ever seen. In a little spermatozoa, in a pretty
little egg without a shell, he has put the great discoverer of
God-consciousness, the one we call man. Look at the
depth of that great organization.

Remember one law which I have learned: Those who do 297
not learn to belong to a man whom they love will never
know the art of belonging to a God whom they will never
know.

There is not a single human being who can write your 298
destiny, except the One Who writes everybody's destiny.

He looks after you and He lives in you. Recognize Him. I 299
assure you, He is in you; you are the manifestation of that
Lord.

Man does not come to this world for benefit. Don't ask for 300
things, be one with the Divine; that is the ultimate cosmic
energy in which you are to merge. When you recite this
mantra it is equal to millions and billions of suns: Ek Ong
Kar Sat Nam Siri Wha Guru. And the day shall come when
you shall have the light within you, light equal to that which
you cannot say. There is no vocabulary and there is no
tongue to say how bright that light is; but remember, that
light you shall see and that is the only light by which you can
overcome the cycle of karmas; then nothing disturbs you.
You live as normal beings, beyond the power of the time
cycle. To stop the cycle you require first to have a charge in
you. You must have power in you; without it, you cannot
stop the cycle of the time. It hits you time and again. It
makes you rich and poor. It makes you healthy and un-
healthy. It makes you great and small. This is the fluctuation
of the time cycle. You go and come, you take another birth;
again you go and come; so it is just a circle and you are
working with it and what do you have to do with it? In this
circle you enter into the other circle. That is all.

Mind

Meditation is the creative control of the self where the In-   301
finite can talk to you.

All talking, all thinking, all thoughts must be pure.   302

Conquer your mind and you will conquer the world.   303
Which mind? The conscious mind? No. The supreme conscious mind? No. Which mind? The subconscious mind. If
you conquer your subconscious mind, then you win the
world.

A relaxed mind is a creative mind and a creative mind is a   304
relaxed mind and only a relaxed mind can become a one-
pointed mind, and a one-pointed mind is the most wonderful mind; it is the most powerful, it can do anything.

Purity of mind is a necessity for man to have supreme   305
spiritual power.

Your totality is only identified as an ego through the mind. 306

If you do not control the thought waves through the will, 307
then the thoughts will flow either from the subconscious
mind or from the creative mind.

When you say, "I am a God-conscious person," it means 308
you realize that your mental capacity is infinity.

Mind is a unit energy given to you to serve you. Be its 309
guide and not its slave.

O mind, you are a part of that universal light; recognize 310
yourself as who you are.

Avatars have come, the teachings have come, the scrip- 311
tures have been there just to teach the human being that
you are the master of the given mind. Don't let the mind
lead you to form habits or you will end up a slave.

The active mind becomes still when you meditate, and the 312
passive mind becomes active. When thoughts come to you,
don't get upset; let them pass through; and when they pass
through just sit and laugh that they are gone. Feel relaxed,
then you will never have dreams. After some time of meditation you will find a time when no thought will be released
by the passive mind. Then you will enjoy a state of bliss.

Begin communicating to your mind. The mind is your   313
friend and is all the time with you. The mind will bring you
the realization of God-consciousness. The mind will give
you deep sleep. The mind will be in your dreams. The mind
is what is seeing and perceiving and talking and hearing.
Your whole world is in the mind.

Everything in you is your mind. That is the pivot of you.   314
Beyond the mind what have you?

When we feel we are limited, we become limited. When   315
we feel we are unlimited, we become unlimited.

This planet Earth is a visiting ground. We are here tem-   316
porarily on a visa. When the visa is up you have got to go.
The law is: As light you came and as light you can go. That
is the condition of the visa. But the load you carry here will
become your own fetters and keep you earthbound. But
the mind which is a part of the Universal Mind with its
thought pattern totally trained and unattached to those
things which are material and earthly—that mind lives in the
attitude of gratitude and will let the soul go.

Man from the very first is a habit-free being and this is a   317
freedom given to him. But as we develop, we slowly develop habits and man becomes so accustomed to habitual
thought patterns that he intellectually justifies them.

You are what you think. Your mental projection is the 318 highest projection in existence in the human body. Any time you mentally think a law, you become a law. There is no problem. Nothing comes from outside.

If you realize that "I am in existence," then you know that 319 your mind is something totally separate from you.

Man must subject his own intellectual thought waves to 320 the guidance of his will.

You must accept that you are you and that your mind is 321 also you. When you have a relationship between you and your mind, it shall answer all problems.

Everything exists. Man has been blessed. These blessings 322 come to a man by a creativity of the mind activity. Mental activity is so powerful that man can block even death.

What is a habit? When the mind is tuned after an activity, 323 it is known as a habit. First you tune the mind into activity and then the habit is established. You become slanderous if the habit is slanderous; you become divine if the habit is divine.

Remember, you have power to the extent that your mind 324
can be pointed on one subject. The mind doesn't have
awareness of anything but the present; the mind follows the
present. These practices which we are giving to you are to
make your mind develop the habit of concentrating. The
secret is how to concentrate your mental energy, and the
moment you know how to concentrate your mental energy,
one thing is past; there shall not be any problems. Problems
exist when man cannot concentrate mental energy and find
his way through.

Anything that is limited cannot compare itself to the 325
Unlimited. That is the difference in this existence. If you
train your mind to understand that you are unlimited, then
every bounty for you is unlimited; and when you train
yourself you are limited, everything is limited for you.

O mind, when you were not born you were with Infinity. 326
You were given this finite body to realize the Infinity in the
finite and you will leave this body to go to that Infinity again.
O mind, again you will be with Infinity, so why are you worried? If God has given you grace, He has given you grace.
When you were a child you were taken care of through certain adverse circumstances and certain favorable circumstances. But through all the circumstances, He took care of
you and brought you to the shore of maturity. Now, when
you are mature, why do you worry?

If at any stage man understands that he is not part of Infin- 327
ity, he is limiting himself. Our mind is nothing but a mirror,
in which the Universal Light, the Cosmos, the Infinity, can
be reflected by our habits and deeds in which we attach
preference to matters on earth. This in the scriptures is
known as the mud of the time. The mud of the time is a
state of mind in which man, over his universal consciousness, gives preference to matters and materials.

What is between the body and the spirit? Mind. 328

When the one-pointed, infinite beam of the mind starts 329
sending the signal into the infinity and the infinity relates to
the finite, the unit becomes united and this is called the
highest stage of the yogic mind.

If you cannot face your subconscious mind, how in God's 330
name are you going to face God?

What are good and bad deeds? A good deed is when we 331
confirm our consciousness, and a bad deed is when we
betray our consciousness. It doesn't matter what our consciousness is, but we must decide, channelize it, and live to
it. There is nothing good and there is nothing bad, but the
thinking makes it so.

We think we die. We think we live. We think we exist. All 332
this thinking is nonfundamental truth.

When the mind cannot relax, then all efforts fail. 333

The soul sees and does not see. The subconscious sees 334
and then it computes and sends its signal to the Supreme
Computer, all the time.

The mind of the being has no limit and no direction. You 335
start thinking anything right now and then change the
thought. Who changes the thought of your mind? It is you.
If you establish the relationship of the one which changes
the mind or the thoughts of the intellect, then your
everything is controlled. And when a person controls his
beam of universal energy, then his mind becomes universal
in experience.

The moment the physical collapses and the soul turns 336
from its physical structure to its astral structure, then the
mind says "Okay, good-bye. I've had enough." Then at
that time, if the mind has the power toward infinity, it grabs
the soul toward infinity. If it has a finite part, then it leads
the soul to that extent. You must remember that the personality is based on your mental self.

Man decides everything, because everything is in his 337
mind. I am a yogi because it is in your mind. If I am a
perfect master it is because it is in your mind. If I am a nut, it
is because it is in your mind. Everything is in your mind.
Nothing else besides that exists with you. You are learning
because it is your mind which is learning. I am teaching
because it is mind that is teaching.

If you are going to be mind alone, then you are doing an 338
injustice to both your mind and your soul. And if you are
calculating everything on the basis of mind, you cannot get
the correct result. You are calculating wrong. The intellect
releases the thought. You must check that thought with the
body and soul, because you are body and soul as well as
mind.

The mind has to be focused in creativity to generate 339
adaptability to total universe. That is what we mean by
creative meditation.

Physics uses the language of symbols. Their symbols are 340
never wrong but their interpretation is sometimes blocked.
But the intuitive mind is different. It gets the message like a
teletype. It gets them clear and does not have to decode.
The intuitive mind acts with solar centers. The psychic acts
with the solar plexus.

Some people say it is all mind and there is no need for 341
body. Well, I will tell you a story. A student came to me and
I said to him, "Take this sword and cut off your neck. Why
do you need this body? Just cut it off and we will communicate on an astral level. If mind is everything then why
don't you do it?" The mind is everything only to those who
have found the Giver of the mind.

Who is that in you that controls the mind? It is called the 342
will of the being. It is also a part of the mind. Mind is like an
onion. It has so many layers. If you peel the onion, you will
find nothing.

The subconscious mind is like a television camera fixed in   343
the brain. It is a part of your mind. It films consciously, it
records you, and you can't get out of it.

You should meditate consciously and talk to your sub-   344
conscious self.

At the judgment time the subconscious tells the story. It   345
has recorded everything and then what can you argue?
How can you argue with yourself? God wants you but you
cannot face Him. So when man is hiding, whom is he hiding from? His subconscious mind. He is hiding from his own
photographer.

Understand that you have to understand yourself; and   346
through the self-understanding you have to experience the
truth, and that will make the mind steady.

Your subconscious mind will not let you go; and if it will   347
not let you go, why don't you prepare yourself now? Is that
too much to ask?

What is the projection of the mind? Is the mind an organ   348
in the body you can just take out? No. Is it the intellect that
gives you a constant stream of thought? No. Is it the individual and his working energy in him? No. Is it the individual? No. Is it God? No. What is it? If you know what it
is, then you know everything. It is the link between your existence reality and your total infinity.

Commanding the mind is only the art of survival in a state 349 of bliss.

The mind is the child that God gave you to have 350 supremacy over time. If you let this mind go free, it is going to give you a hell of a time. Our best friend and the most beautiful child that we have is the mind. When it is innocent, it smiles and does its job. Then the mind becomes an adult. Then it wants to marry, so it gets married to maya and gets confused and forgets you totally.

If you do not have a mastery of your mind you cannot 351 know the mystery of existence.

When the individual consciousness controls the sub- 352 conscious mind, then the universal mind is experienced.

When the subconscious mind is controlled consciously by 353 the individual as a habit and he does not relate to his negative past as a habit and he relates to infinite nature to bless him, that person reaches the highest consciousness as a living being. In the occult science he is known as *jiwan mukti*. Mukti means "salvation," mukti means "through with karma cycle," and jiwan means "alive."

We are always related to our mind. The moment we 354 relate to our soul, our mind becomes our servant. When the mind becomes our servant, the whole of nature serves us.

You have your conscious mind and your subconscious. If   355
you can control your subconscious consciously, you are a
conscious person. When you consciously control your subconscious, you become your master.

The mind can be controlled by two methods. The mind   356
follows breath and breath is the tender charge of God. To
control your mind through breath you can definitely still
yourself.

You may follow a saint or a yogi or a perfect master, give   357
him all your wealth, put ash on your head, go to the top of
a mountain, and kill yourself. It's not going to work out
because the only freedom you can have consciously is the
freedom from your subconscious mind and your subconscious mind records you. All your deeds are recorded by
your subconscious mind. Depression in personality comes
because depression in consciousness comes first. The subconscious mind has the power to block the flow of the
energy from the astral body. Huge universal energy is
there, 11,000 volts, but you have 110.

Depression in consciousness is the real cause of your fluc-   358
tuation. Your error is not caused because you can cause an
error; error happens because you have an error in consciousness, a dent in your consciousness. You are not consciously conscious of your existence; therefore, you are not
consciously conscious of your activity; therefore, you are
not consciously conscious of your action; therefore, you are
not consciously conscious of your reaction. And when you
are not consciously conscious of what action you are taking
and what sequence it will lead to, you are also not willing to
accept the reaction. When you are not willing to accept the
reaction, depression has to happen.

Thought is the projected wavelength of the mind; intellect 359
is the common source in the universe; so if you can feed
that intellect to the common source, you can direct your
thought wave into the thought wave of any other such
source. This means that an individual can control the
thought wave of an individual at any spot on the planet
Earth. Not only do you control the thought, you even control the action. Not only do you control the action, you control the destiny.

There is only one difference between the animal and the 360
human animal: Your mind has a power of infinity, whereas
the animal does not have that. That is the difference; otherwise, everything is equal. The animal is alive, you are alive.
The animal eats, you eat. He eliminates, you eliminate. He
cleans with the tongue, you clean with the shower. It
doesn't make a difference. But the fact remains, your mind
is beyond time, his mind is subject to time because his instincts are subject to time. If he wants to have a mating
season he has to wait for spring, you don't have to. You
want a mating season, you don't even care about normal
social courtesies. That's the way you are, because your instincts are under your control; his instincts are under the
control of time. That's the only difference between you and
the animal.

You communicate with you. Your mind communicates 361
with your mind. Now you have to understand which mind
because your mind communicates with your mind. One
mind is the mind of the intellect and senses, the other mind

is that which observes what the mind of the intellect is doing. We call it consciousness.

The intellectual mind created what? Thought. Thought 362
created what? Emotion. Emotion created what? Desire. Desire created what? The object, the act.

The war of the senses is the higher sense, the higher con- 363
sciousness, and the individual consciousness. The finite and infinite consciousness are always at war. There is no ending to it. It will never end.

You have a policeman in you and that policeman is above 364
you and is paid by none other than the almighty Creator, and we call that Creator in the scientific terminology today the subconscious mind. You cannot hide any action, any thought from the subconscious mind. The subconscious mind records you and he bothers you. He bothers you at night when you are sleeping through your dreams; he takes away all your nervous energy and leaves you with nothing.

Breaking the barriers of the subconscious mind is the 365
union of the unit consciousness with supreme consciousness; you must not have any misunderstanding about yoga. When the conscious mind can break through the barriers of the subconscious block and can penetrate and merge with the supreme conscious mind, that union is known as yoga, a happening, and we seek this happening because the finite must know its infinite potential.

What is a guilt consciousness? When you are conscious of 366
not doing something, but you do it; a guilty conscience is
nothing but consciously doing something which consciously
you are aware you should not do. We call it subconscious
blocks. Between the conscious existence and the super-
conscious there is a subconscious. When there are a lot of
blocks in the subconscious mind, the conscious works as a
conscience, the supreme conscious works as a supreme
conscience, and in between there is no communication.

Microconsciousness should be balanced with macrocon- 367
sciousness. The imbalance between microconsciousness
and macroconsciousness is known as the human tragedy.

One has to be very conscious in dealing with one's own 368
mind. The best way is not to record any activity for which
your subconscious mind can pick at you. Secondly, never
do anything which you cannot explain to yourself and
prove to yourself on the touchstone of Universal Truth.
Third, never take any action for which you cannot face the
reaction, because the first thing to give you reaction will be
your own subconscious mind. Fourth, never compromise
with your lower nature, with a friend of lower intention, of
negative intention, or of negative environment. Make your
will rise at primal hours and repeat the primal sound which
means the word of the beginning, because if the word of the
beginning is true, then you are true.

The mind is not subject to time and place. The mind can- not be subject to time and place, but there is a relationship of mind and body. If you have the technical know-how and you use that technique, mind and body can become one. The moment you can bring mind and body into one, then there is only one alternative left. When mind and body become one, then universality and creativity of the self can be recognized. This is very important.

Realization

A*nanda*, bliss, is a constant state of mind where one does   370
not feel disturbed either by gain or by loss.

The problem on this planet today is that there is so much   371
knowledge around us we are unable to select what is right
and what is wrong. Not only do we not know what is right
and what is wrong, there is a basic problem, a fundamental
problem. All we want to know is philosophy, but we don't
want to change. And I assure you, philosophy does not
change a man totally. Philosophy is the most useless thing
on the earth, just as a teacher who also does not change a
person is also a very hopeless teacher.

They say that he who gives enjoys and he who takes is a   372
beggar. That is why they say: If you want to learn knowledge, beg it and beg it so in pity and mercy that out of the
giver of knowledge God may come.

A principle in life to remember is to travel light. You are   373
traveling all the time. Travel light, live light, spread the light,
be the light.

The mind is very important, but the body is equally important, and the soul is equally important. That trinity is a totality.   374

Actually, to be very honest, we do not know how powerful we are. The teacher inspires our power. The guru/teacher is a servant. The teacher is a slave and a servant to God-consciousness. His job is to inspire the man who studies with him, so that the man realizes realization through his own realization.   375

Our existence is nothing but consciousness. If our existence is nothing but consciousness, where is the difficulty? The difficulty is that we are not conscious of our consciousness.   376

If you can sacrifice your limited ego, you will always get in return an unlimited spirit; and when you get an unlimited spirit the universe serves you.   377

Those who continue to live in the past always throw their future into the gutter. Those who live to their word are honored in the court of the world, and those who do not are not honored.   378

"Angel" is a transparent guidance manufactured out of compassion in God-consciousness.   379

Live as royal saints. Nobody shall walk over you, but nobody who needs you shall be deprived of your strength.   380

There is a law of the golden chain. Whatever you shall do 381
to me, however you shall treat me as a teacher, so others
will treat you. If you shall do it to me, it shall be done to
thee. When you say, *I can do it* or *I cannot do it*, you are
fooling yourself. Instead you should say, as is the Will of the
Divine, it is being tried through me. If I am successful it is his
grace; if not, it is his Will. How much a man understands
God is measured by this realization.

When the little me has recognized the big me and the little 382
i has recognized the big I, oneness is achieved. And when
one knows that he is the one and one knows everything is
one, then what is there to find? It is only when we think that
I am and everything else is everything else that we have to
find something.

Don't cause a cause for which you are not willing to have 383
the effect. Sequence shall lead to consequence, so don't
build that sequence whose consequence you are not willing
to face.

Words do not mean anything. If someone starts arguing 384
that which is wrong, if you know it is wrong, just say yes, it
is wrong. Get out of it. You can learn about you from
everywhere. A person who can accept facts about himself is
a factual man.

What is a great soul? A great soul is one who recognizes 385
all other souls. A universal soul is that which has merged
with every soul. There is a very delicate difference.

Those who dye their hearts in the concept of God divine and live in the color of white light and righteousness, those who merge in that eternal light, do not remain with their remains and their balances.   386

When you know that all is light, then you are enlightened. What is enlightened? When you recognize the light. Where? Within you.   387

You belong to only one thing, and that is Truth; and you have got to be delivered to only one thing, and that is Truth.   388

You are true now, you were true then, and you shall ever be true—that is all you have to know, and you will be free.   389

Consciousness is a gift of your Creator. If you rob your own consciousness, then nothing will be left with you, and when you leave this world you will leave in misery and agony.   390

A bus driver is the best example of a guru. He is totally involved in taking you to a destination, but he is uninvolved with you as well. His job is to pick you up and to deliver you.   391

The fundamental truth is to realize, to feel, and to experience life within you. We normally feel and experience life within us in relationship to environments; so we feel en-   392 vironments, not life. One who experiences life experiences the source of life. One who experiences the source of life knows infinity, and that person knows the past, present, and future.

You have to realize that you are the center of your own mental psyche. 393

Behave constantly and strive on the path of righteousness, giving your total self unto the fire of purity and maintaining the flame of light to the end; your karma will be done, giving will be complete, blessings will exist, awareness will be thy gift. That is the rightful right of every man. That is the truth in you. 394

Compassion is nothing but realization of adjustable values. Nobody is bad. If one does not act or understand well, or he is limited, you should have compassion, not negativity. Why does somebody harm you? Why does somebody slander you? Because he doesn't know any better. 395

We have to understand the basic fundamental existence of ours—to understand the spirit. Once you understand the spirit you are all right. 396

Life is a constant vibration. It is a magnetic field which is active constantly. It relates to the universal magnetic field, just as gears grind together. 397

When creative meditation is achieved, knowledge 398
becomes understood because it becomes a practical thing.
Every sound, every word that somebody speaks to you,
you will understand if your mind is tuned creatively and has
a meditative form in it; then you will understand what truth
is and what nontruth is. Otherwise, things do not have
meaning for you at all. In your whole life your biggest con-
fusion is when somebody talks to you and you do not know
what he is saying to you and to what extent he means it and
to what extent he does not.

It does not take centuries of practice and incarnations of 399
study to know what truth is. We all know what truth is.

The freedom of instinct exists with man and not in the 400
vegetable or animal world. Why? Because you have a
chance to find your soul.

We confine ourselves. We are slaves to rituals, we are 401
slaves to understanding, we are prisoners of our thoughts.
We call them concepts. Think of your slavery and your
chains. No one can put you in prison but yourself. You are
slaves to sex, to desire, to food. You are slaves to your way
of life. You are afraid to face anybody with your originality.
You are more afraid of truth than of life.

Saints and sages have come to show the path to man, but 402
we forget the path and get into the dogma.

All training and all knowledge is meant for only one pur- 403
pose, and the purpose is very simple and clear: that you
may be in a position to control your mental self as well as
your physical self.

The Creator has made the creation so that it might rival the 404
Creator.

Something must be done to experience the infinity in this 405
finite form. In this finite form the body has been given to
you to experience infinity. That is the only purpose of God.

When you practice religion you forget to relate to origin 406
and you stick to rituals, and the message of the soul is totally forgotten.

Spirituality and Godhead does not mean that if I meditate 407
all the time I am very spiritual. Spirituality does mean that I
am perfect in my spirit as far as my relationship is concerned
on all levels of consciousness.

What is in this universe and in this total cosmos that is 408
beyond time? The Truth. Truth is beyond time, everything
else is in time; and when you are Truth you are beyond
time.

People want to demonstrate power, and that is a sickness 409
which even God cannot cure. It is beyond curing, and they
call it "spiritual ego." When a man becomes a little spiritual
and people start loving him and respecting him, giving him
things, bowing to him, well, that's where the problem starts.
His brain—which understands that he walks on the earth,
that he is a humble man, a creature created by God—forgets all that. He becomes a balloon. He blows up and he
starts talking and behaving and feeling that everybody is just
nothing and he is everything, that he is the wisest of the
wise.

The path of the saint is this: "Man, you are a god within 410
yourself; go, recognize it."

What is Truth? Your very existence is Truth. Not to 411
recognize your grace in existence and seeking things outside you is maya. Gurus say, Don't have maya, don't run
after maya. For you, good food is a maya, a good house is
a maya, good clothing is a maya, a good bed is a maya.
Maya is not recognizing the Truth.

Three mantras you should never say: (1) I don't know. (2) 412
I'm not ready. (3) I can't do it.

What is consciousness? And who are you? You are con- 413
sciousness. We are a part of the universal consciousness,
and the exact meaning of consciousness is reality. The total

creativity of the reality principle we have folded into one word: *consciousness*. It has no sadness of death, it has no happiness of birth, it has no merit or demerit of existence. When you are conscious, you know it as it is.

Beauty is in the eyes of the beholder, and everyone has 414
his own aspect of beauty and he is contributing, as is the whole universe. The plants, the animals, the birds, the human beings, they all contribute to universal beauty; that is a creative concept, a creative meditation.

What is a fear complex? When you feel limited. If you 415
feel that you are a part of the universe and the universe is a part of you, what is there to fear?

The greatest miracle is unity. 416

A holy man is one who sees sinner and saint alike. Saints 417
are those who have the greatest compassion; a human being on the path of righteousness who has compassion is a saint.

There is only one way to live. This is very confusing   418
because many people say there are many men and many
paths. But there is only one way and there is only one path
and there is only one God and there is only one way to
reach Him and there is only one truth to know and there is
only one humanity to practice one-pointedness of mind—
that is righteousness. Whether you are a Christian, a Jew, a
Buddhist, or anything, it doesn't make any difference. So
long as you are a human being, you have to understand
one thing: Either you play in the hand of circumstances or
you make the circumstances play in your hand.

Any man who can meditate, relate, concentrate, and   419
imagine in inaction or action that he belongs to Infinity is
beautiful.

How are saints produced? The first sign of a saint is that   420
he is original, he is what he is.

There are men who have changed the face of this earth   421
and there are men that are not known by twenty people.
Both are men. There is no difference between a man and a
man. But if a man has gathered his total activity and created
an infinity in activity, we call him a great man. Some men
are limited and some are not, but both are men. Both are
human beings. The human being is infinite; potentially infinite, finite in activity.

Liberation is not that from this Earth you will go to God's   422
kingdom. The kingdom of God is where you are, and
liberation here is when you are a carefree and frank being.

What are you doing on the planet earth? We are here to   423
realize ourselves and nothing more. That's it.

Your total life is nothing without activity. When you are   424
not acting, you are dead. You act in sleep also. You act
through dreams. You act through mental vibrations. You
are continually vibrating. The moment you don't vibrate
you are dead. Death is nothing but nonvibration of a finite
unit. That's all death is.

Saints and sages have more trouble than a normal per-   425
son, because a normal person can sneak his way through;
the saintly man gets stuck. If he has to walk into the fire,
then he has to walk into the fire. But why then doesn't he
get burned? Do you know why? Because he feels he is the
creature of the Creator; and when you feel you are the
creature of the Creator, then the cause does not give you
the effect. Do everything in the name of the activity. Work
your way through in the name of your Creator. It is a relationship which you have to mentally establish. It is also
known as transcendental meditation.

Self-exertion or self-reliance and self-realization is not   426
possible for everybody. Why not? Because we don't think
we are part of infinity and infinity is a part of us. We do not
recognize the very divinity in us. That a creature has been
created and that this creation has a purpose is totally forgotten by man.

Minds have no equality. Some are very intellectual, some   427
are very practical, some are very positive, and some are
negative. But one thing is common—the soul.

To be spiritual is to give and give, never to expect back, as 428
clouds give rain and never come down to take the water
back. And your life exists on that giving. There is nothing to
learning to be spiritual; learn from the clouds that give you
the light and the spirit of giving through their own drops of
water which create huge vegetation for you.

Those who do not love to eat vegetables love to eat those 429
who do eat vegetables. I wonder why they have to put
those creatures into agony.

If one will realize God, then he will become God. What is 430
realization? When you become that which you realize.

Because you carry scriptures on your back like a donkey, 431
you think you are a wise man. So long as scriptures come
only on your tongue, so long as they do not come from
your soul, you are kidding yourself.

It is ridiculous to tell you not to drink, don't do this, don't 432
do that, and have no substitute for it. It's terrible, it is not
honest. You must find the nectar inside, and if you don't, a
person has no right to tell you, "Don't do this." It is against
the natural principle of a human being that he should be
told not to do anything.

The world never mourned Gandhi's death, it mourned for 433
that symbolic peace he was living in. Nobody mourns for
anybody; all we mourn for is that cavity which happens.

The human being is actually meant not to be limited. Then 434
the question arises, why does the human being experience
hurdles, limitations, and being limited? The answer is very
simple. The human being has never learned to live as a
human being. The human being is limited because the
human being has never experienced his own self.

It is a simple thing: When you are attached, how can you 435
be universal?

The sexual act is nothing, but it is a possibility of 436
establishing a foundation for the next generation.

At this moment your existence is secure and granted by 437
the entire beauty of this universe. And I see myself shining
with that glitter with which I see the sun, the moon, and the
stars. The whole planet Earth shines with exactly the same
radiance, and I am a part of it, and it is a part of me. And I
know it is all temporary. Earth has given me a vehicle for
staying on it, and I am beyond the vehicle. The day I have
to leave, that vehicle has to be left back on this earth,
deposited in its bosom safely and securely.

It is a normal thing in human behavior to be selfish. You 438
can't get away from it, but you can channel it. Be selfish to
the extent of being known as generous. Cater to the image
to be selflessly serviceful to others.

What is a Christian? A Christian is someone who raises 439
himself above the five elements as the master did it. Jesus
did it, that is why he is Christ.

The moment the being realizes that he is a complete being, 440 this is a stage of ecstasy. When a human being, a man, realizes he is a man, it is an ecstasy in itself; and when a youth realizes he is young, it is an ecstasy in itself; and when an old man realizes his experience of age, it is an ecstasy in itself. But when a seventy-year-old man wants to act like a sixteen-year-old boy, where is the ecstasy?

You go to college, you study, you graduate, and then you 441 walk out into your life. But when you go to a spiritual teacher you become a leech, you stick to him. This is not the way; learn from the spiritual teacher. Practice and develop your life. The only way one should reach spirituality is to become fearless. If you are fearful, then you are not learning. If God is infinity and you realize God-consciousness and then you realize infinity, then you do not fear.

A guru is a consciousness and not a person. This should 442 not be misunderstood.

Every individual has the potential to be original. 443

The concept of beautiful and ugly is an individual concept. 444

How many people live in reality? The answer is 2 per- 445 cent. And where does the other 98 percent live? In a dream.

What is the destiny of man? To project gracefully through 446 existence. That is your destiny: You must project grace through your existence.

Your deeds should be honorable and they cannot be hon- 447
orable if you do not have honorable intentions. It is the
honorable intention that will bring the honorable act from
you.

We come on this earth to go. We come in grace; 448
therefore, we must go in grace. This is the highest power
one has to achieve.

We are consciouslessly conscious and if we are con- 449
sciously conscious not to be negative, we are levitated.

There is individual consciousness and from there, group 450
consciousness and then we reach universal consciousness.
The aim of man is to reach universal consciousness.

When you ignore the truth, you will be ignored; any per- 451
son who can ignore the truth or true advice shall be truthfully ignored by the Supreme Existence, because truth is
supreme.

I do not know how I exist, but still I am existing, and this is 452
the wonder of reality. And this whole realization came to
me when I uttered one little sound: Wha, wha, wha.

Life has a message for everyone. Life provides an oppor- 453
tunity for everyone. Fortunate are those who avail themselves of it, unfortunate are those who miss it.

Man has the right to change his destiny and man can change his destiny. Life can be changed beyond dreams, beyond expectations, but we do not trust life. 454

What is success? Success is when you are faced with something and you accomplish it. Then you are known as successful. 455

You run after wealth and glory and glamour. But it will run after you, providing you are an open channel. 456

There is no way out. There is only one way and that is for the individual to relate to his consciousness consciously. 457

Make your temple clean. Make your heart open with love so that He can come and sit in it. Whosoever lives in fear has not seen the light. We have forgotten who we are. We are one and there is One to whom we belong. The aim of life is to inspire each other to God-consciousness. 458

Sacrifice is total nonpresence of the I. 459

Never misunderstand or understand that as human beings you have something different from other human beings, except values. 460

The Creator created the creature to realize the state of the stability, the finite of the infinity. 461

You have the right to be crazy. You have the right to be 462
wise. I am not challenging your right. You can be secure or
you can be insecure. You can be happy, you can be unhappy. You can earn and live gracefully and you can earn
and live ungracefully. Nobody is challenging that right.
They call it free will because the instinct of the man is in his
control. He has the power of free will.

What is sin? Sin is making or creating a block in the sub- 463
conscious mind.

The highest charity is to die for truth. Go we must, there is 464
nothing wrong in going; as we have come, we must go.

There is nothing before commitment, there is nothing be- 465
yond commitment, because commitment is complete within
itself.

You don't need to be spiritual, you need not be holy, you 466
need not study under a great master. You aren't required to
follow anybody, you aren't required to be with anybody,
you aren't required to learn anything, if—it's a big if—if you
know who you are, and not only know, but realize who you
are.

The coming times, the Age of Aquarius, through which we 467
are all going to pass, will be an age of peace and an age of
wisdom and an age of knowledge. It will be an age of san-
ity, not insanity.

One must be conscious to have consciousness, and one must be conscious that his conscious energy can always vibrate in the direction which is righteous. 468

For every problem there is an answer. No question can exist without the answer being already in it. For instance, ask any question. 469
Question: What is infinity?
Answer: Infinity is what.
The moment you ask what, you are relating something beyond the finite and you are in infinity.

All human beings have one thing in common. The breath of life is one common thing. 470

To be calm is the highest achievement of the self. 471

Everything is within the man, nothing is outside of him. 472

You are dead because you're not alive to your consciousness. But when you face the sequence and relate it to the consequence and then surmount the consequences, you become alive. 473

Trust only comes when you trust yourself. When you trust your dignity, you will always be dignified. When you trust your love, you will always be lovable. When you trust your beauty, you will always be beautiful. When you trust your greatness, you will always be great. 474

Polarity

I remember when Mahatma Gandhi was imprisoned in a   475
jail. When he was released, he requested, "Can I stay one
week more?" They asked what kind of guy is he? He said,
"It is a very big jail; there are a lot of people here and I
have been teaching a special course on meditation that will
take a week more to finish. If I am extended a week, I can
teach these people and I'll be grateful if you allow me to stay
in here." The superintendent said, "We will charge you four
rupees, half a dollar a day for that week if you want to stay;
otherwise, you better get out, we don't need you any-
more." Can you believe that kind of consciousness? His
consciousness was that he never felt imprisoned.

How can your Creator and how can Mother Nature who   476
created you make you lonely? There are beautiful trees,
there are beautiful times; everywhere around you beauty is
in such abundance that if you look ahead, you can enjoy
and enjoy forever and ever. Why do you feel lonely? And
why do you want to be recognized? And why do you over-
extend yourself and make yourself weak?

You have a consciousness in you, and if you do not know 477
that you are a balance of two polarities and if you do not relate to both your polarities, you are not relating to a reality.

For those who have found the truth, today is tomorrow, 478
and today is also yesterday.

The institution of marriage is two polarities joined together 479
to pull life together through hard and even times. But now-
adays we think of relationship as staying together through
even times only. How can it be possible that through any
relationship you cannot have hard and even times?

If you can sacrifice your limited ego, you will always get in 480
return unlimited spirit.

You make habits and then habits make you. If you have 481
any habit, you will be a slave of that habit. This is the slavery of man. Liberation is the state beyond habits.

First man wants money, then money man wants power, 482
then powerful man wants peace of mind.

What is the difference between a man of God-con- 483
sciousness and an individual man? Men of God-
consciousness are three people at the same time. Men of
self-consciousness are also three people at the same time.
The man of God-consciousness has God, his guru, and
himself. The man of self-consciousness has himself, his
ego, and his desire. It is a question of being limited and
unlimited.

124

Cavity in consciousness is a duality. We act, but we know   484
we do not think that way. Or we think one way and act
another, and this duality, this split in the consciousness is
sin.

One act of forgiveness can make you God. One act of in-   485
tolerance can make you an ordinary man. A little charity
can make you a giver, which is the tradition of God. And if
you steal a few dollars you can relate only to your animal
nature. A little sacrifice can give you back your consciousness, which is divine. A little greed will give back your animal nature.

Times will change, values will change; only one thing does   486
not change—that is the depth in you, the soul within you,
the part of you which is immortal. A mortal changes, an immortal does not change.

There are two ways of living in this world, the way of   487
worry and the way of relaxation. If you worry, you have to
concentrate to imagine and it becomes physical work; but if
you turn your mind to the universal mind, then things will
come to you.

All things must be balanced. Each day of life is another   488
day of death.

It is better to die while speaking the truth than to live as a   489
coward.

Ugliness has its place. Ugliness serves because ugliness is 490 only that which by comparison promotes beauty. Who are you to condemn it? Who are you to judge it? Because of a fear complex you see ugliness around you and you see it in yourself; this brings a fear complex.

Any man who creates environments to show clarity about 491 the causes and effects of the Creator—beauty and bounty in this world—gets merged into infinity.

In the lowest of the low lives the highest of the high, and 492 you who would walk on the path of awareness must know that, fundamentally, in your humility lies grace, in your firmness lies your truth.

When life is lived, everything comes to you, but when 493 you live life then you have to struggle for everything.

One who experiences the fact that life is a vibration, that 494 life is a come and go, such a man is an enlightened man. He is the one who is liberated.

Life is a book of changes. It should be read only to 495 understand how it works. You can't help the changes in life; they must come whether they are good or bad because the good must follow the bad and the bad must follow the good.

Those who do not know how to obey will never learn how to command. Those who are not perfect students can never be perfect teachers. Those who do not give can never get. Life has a balance and polarity. If you go to the North Pole, then you are just opposite to the South Pole. 496

The more spiritual you become the harder times you experience; the more spiritual you become, the more slandered you are. 497

There are two levels of communication: one, when the unit talks to Infinity, and two, when Infinity talks to the unit. 498

Your existence is truth, and that is God; but when you don't realize it, that is maya. 499

What causes pain in our life is that we do not know how to live as relaxed beings. When you are not relaxed, the spirit will not prevail through you. If you are not relaxed, you are unable to communicate and you cannot understand, so you don't live. There are two ways of living: living and existing. When you exist, you don't live; when you live, then you exist in a graceful manner. 500

There is a difference between a carefree man and a careless man. Carelessness is a deficiency, it happens because of laziness. You don't put forth proper effort. To be carefree is to use your higher mind. You do your best. You feel good and keep up. Let the results be with God. 501

I am not worried about how you feel, I am only worried 502
about one thing, that you *do* feel. A neutral attitude is the
joy of God.

Asking for self-reliance and obtaining self-reliance is not 503
only great, it is the answer to *every* problem of life. No one
is so small that he cannot be great.

There cannot be *shanti** without *shakti.** * Peace cannot 504
be if you do not have your nerve standardness. You cannot
be content if you do not have your vitality. So, in any case
you must build in yourself the power of righteousness; then
you can lead yourself to righteousness.

In this world, we know that matter cannot be produced, 505
cannot be destroyed. Somebody is rich, somebody is poor.
Somebody is fat, somebody is thin. Somebody is tall,
somebody is short. This world is nothing but a balance. Its
very existence is based on balance. This planet and the entire existence on this planet cannot exist without this great
balance. There is nothing you can add; there is nothing you
can subtract from it.

Hatred is self-suicide and love is self-sacrifice. 506

What is the value of old age? Grace. Any old man who is 507
graceful will be loved and respected. What is the value of
childhood? Sharpness.

*Peace, nothingness
* *Activity, creativity

In all darkness, there is a light and in all light there is a   508
darkness.

The Piscean motto is: *I believe* and *I shall know*. But the   509
Aquarian motto is: *I know* and *I shall believe*.

Who is the savior? It is your own higher consciousness   510
which can save you from your own lower consciousness.

This world has a phenomenon. They always call reality   511
nonreality, and nonreality reality.

The moment your polarity brings to you your totality,   512
there cannot be any other vibration but harmony.

What is God union? It is the same union that we find in   513
our polarity. In that ecstasy, in that enjoyment where there
is a complete merger of two polarities, when the female of-
fers herself and the male accepts, both unite in that ecstasy
of infinity. In such a union a soul is born out of the soul of a
woman, which changes the face of this earth.

It is not only the child that is born which is creativity, it is the   514
merger of the two polarities that is highly important.

When the polarities are not merged, physical intercourse   515
between a man and a woman is nothing but an exploitation.

Faith means one-pointedness of mind toward Infinity. Du- 516
ality means one-pointedness of mind toward two existen-
ces, Infinite and finite.

Work is a workshop. Those who work to glorify the crea- 517
tivity of the Creator, those are the blessed beings. The life of
the householder is the highest of all lives. And what is a
householder but a total union of positive and negative, of
moon and sun, of Purusha and maya,* of male and female, of yin and yang.**

If the being has not realized that giving is giving by itself and 518
its greatness is unlimited, he has not enjoyed the essential
thing.

Giving does not mean cleverness. Giving is not giving 519
when you feel you are losing something. Giving in reality is
creating an effective vacuum, sucking the flow from the
great Infinite Consciousness. That is giving.

There are three values: Feel good, be good, and do good. 520

Not having the flexibility to change is a tragedy in itself; 521
and having too much flexibility not to stand for anything is a
tragedy in itself.

*Creator and Creation
**Polarities of existence

130

The Almighty God is very weak before the man of God. It 522 is the law of polarity. The mightiest must be very weak somewhere; if that rule applies to us, it applies to Him. He is omnipresent, omniscient, whatever He is, but He is very weak before his own image.

Nothing is good and nothing is bad, but thinking makes it 523 so. Virtuous are those thieves who have stolen the Nam, bounty of the Name, and have filled themselves so much that they live free from all bondages.

Everything you do is to get recognition. When you don't 524 get recognition, it brings frustration and with frustration comes insecurity and that's what your reality is. You must be recognized, but you have to know how to get recognized. You must learn the technique; and when you are known to be a universal man, you are a man of merit, you are a man of truth, you are a man of compassion, you are like a sky which covers everybody. You are recognized by everybody, not by slandering people, not by negating people. When you become what you really are, then everything shall recognize you. Then you may hide in a closet, people will find you.

Nothing is everything and everything is nothing. When 525 you become nothing, but tune into everything, then everything straightens out.

Everything that comes has to go. Coming and going is a 526 law of life that nothing is going to stop. No, nothing can stop it and nothing should stop it. If my son has to die, he has to die, he should die. All I can say is he should die gracefully.

Where there is a light there is always a shade of polarity; 527
whenever you are very righteous and doing a right job, you
will always end up on a cross or in a gas chamber. It is not
something that is unknown to man in his life, but you must
have dignity and you must have realization of your potential
up to infinity; that what one cannot imagine to hear and
think and see, the other one can show, prove, and do.

Some people think that a holy man is a skinny man with a 528
stick in his hand and a bowl of rice which he eats once a
month, that he lives anywhere, he is never angry. That's
not true. A holy man is a wholesome, compassionate person.

You think a thief is unholy? He maintains the police, fire 529
maintains the fire brigade. Everything has a polarity and in
these polarities, whenever you can create a natural stage,
you are very, very happy, very, very healthy, and very,
very holy. If you have the ability to create this stability, that
is all you need.

We all know what is right, the problem is we do not act 530
for it. We cannot act because we do not have the experience; we do not have the nerves to stand for
righteousness.

If you want to relate to happiness, then get ready for 531
sadness also, because the world is a balance; it is like the cycle of day and night.

If you want to grow, you must face opposition. If you say 532
there will not be people to negate you and not to oppose
you and not to put you down, you can never progress. You
must have equal opposition to the amount you have to in-
crease.

Actually, the thing man does is live for society, forgetting 533
that he is society. The thing you must do is be you, so that
society can be society.

Hell and heaven are right here. In heaven, people live 534
very still, they speak truth, and they are very compassionate. In hell, they jump around, they speculate, and they
fluctuate; their words are never trustable because they don't
trust their own words.

It's very important for you to understand the game of the 535
head and the heart. When the heart is involved, the head
must decide; when the head is involved, the heart must
decide. If you miss either way you will miss the bus of life.

If you don't relate to the past, that is a victory for the 536
future.

Life means death, death means life. There is no dif- 537
ference. You die every day. Every day all of you must die
to live.

When you want to take, you have to learn to give. When 538
you are born, you have to be ready to die.

POLARITY

Life is hooked on a two-edged sword; high and low, good 539
and bad.

It does not matter who you are, it only matters how you 540
radiate. Happiness does not come through materials, it
comes through happiness.

Self is your now and now is your future. 541

There are two ways of living. There are people who han- 542
dle situations and there are people who are handled by
situations.

Levitation is when you look at anything and you are not in 543
it. You hate, but you are not in the hatred. You love, but
you are not in the love. You speak, but you are not in the
speech. You are silent, but you are not in the silence. You
in action is not you in direction.

The law of changes has to be understood. Everybody has 544
to change, everybody changes in the consciousness. When
the student changes he needs more and the teacher should
give him more, and when the teacher finds he cannot give
him more he should direct him to somewhere else where he
can get more. Some teachers are leeches, they stick to their
students.

The truth is that a person never dies and the truth also is 545
that a person never is alive. This is known as polarity of
consciousness.

134

If you have harmony with nature, you will be exalted; if 546
you fight it, you will be consumed.

This life as a whole has a question and an answer and this 547
life as a whole has an existence and a nonexistence. You
exist, but you don't. You have some merits and some
values and you have no merits and no values. You are effective and you are ineffective.

When hell and heaven, praise and slander all become 548
one, this is when faith comes.

Before this life where were you? You don't know. After 549
this life where are you going to go? You don't know.
Whence you came, I don't know. Where you are going, I
don't know. Why do you need to know now? If you don't
need to know now, everything will become known to you
because things are in polarity.

Who is a teacher? The answer is, he who is the best stu- 550
dent is the best teacher.

You die, but you never die; you are alive, but you are 551
never alive.

If someone accepts me as a God, he will see God in me. If 552
someone should accept me as a devil, he will see the devil
in me. But he is the one who is going to see, I am not. Why
should I worry? But, if someone tells me I am a devil and I
tell him that I am not and he is, then I am a real devil; then
the devil comes out in me. There is a devil in me and there
is a God in me; the question is what comes out of me.

There are two kinds of protection, natural protection and 553
individual protection. Natural protection is when the God
protects you and individual protection is by your own
hands.

Either you drive your own car or a chauffeur drives it for 554
you. You have a choice in this world. If you are a great person you have infinity in you, love is in you, your jobs will be
done. Have either faith or a struggle; do it yourself, but consciousness is righteousness.

When you deny something, actually you are accepting 555
those things very deep in your subconscious mind, and
sometimes, when you accept something, you are rejecting
it in your subconscious mind so strongly even you do not
know it. So it is not by your acts that you approve or disap-
prove things. Your personality, which is a known personality, can be known by acts; but your unknown personality is
also there. Man is both unknown and known. Unknown is
divine, known is the individual, however you are denying
God. God is only denied because you say it is unknown. To
know thyself is to know God. God is what? God is a totality,
and when one knows the totality of one's personality, one is
God.

God exalts the lowliest of the low and exalts him to the   556
highest of the high to prove his existence.

The difference between animal and man is not that he   557
walks on four legs and you walk on two; the difference between animal and man is that your instincts are under your
control. An animal's instincts are not under his control. That
is the difference.

What is carbon? Nothing. After thousands of years it   558
becomes a solid crystal. What is the value of a crystal?
Nothing, not much, but when it comes to a gem cutter, he
cuts it and brings out of it a clean and pure crystal carbon
which we call diamond. Then, if you ask its price, it is quite
a bit. This is the state of the human being. If one has not
crystallized himself in the essence of his intelligence and
does not shine through all the facets of his personality, the
price of the human being is zero.

For every beautiful thing, you have to pass through a   559
valley of hardship. There is no liberation without labor.
There is no freedom which is free. To create in you the
power to create the intelligence which will give you power
to be effective in your own living and give you satisfaction in
your own joy, you have to work for it, you have to earn it.

Ego is nothing but a committed consciousness and when   560
your existence is a committed consciousness and your activity is not committed, then there is a duality.

Of God you are the polarity. God is infinite and you are 561
finite.

In Canada, one of the interviewers said to me, "What is the 562
proof that you are a yogi? I want the proof that you are a
yogi. Is it written on your forehead that you are a yogi?" I
said, "I do not have to give proof. The very fact that you ask
me three times, that you doubt that I am a yogi, is the
answer in itself. You are in doubt, I am not. If I am not, it
doesn't matter to me; if I am, it doesn't matter to you." He
said, "I don't understand." I replied, "What you don't
understand, I understand." He said, "Will you just tell me
what makes you believe that you are a yogi?" I said, "My
belief not to rebut you makes me a yogi, and your belief to
rebut me and to corner me makes you an interviewer."

There is no future for those who relate to the past all the 563
time, because the past is now and the future is now. You
can wipe out yesterday; now you can figure out tomorrow.
The activity to live now is called the highest achievement.

Why can't you withdraw within yourself? The moment 564
you go in, the light will go out because action has a reaction, equal and opposite. If you can understand the mystery
of living, you can surmount time; otherwise, time will do
what time has to do.

It is a universal law that one follows the other; but what we 565
want is one, and what we don't want is the other. As rain is
followed by sunshine, tragedy is followed by blessings, and
blessings are followed by tragedy. It is a cycle. If you don't
want blessings, don't want tragedies. If you want tragedies,
want blessings also, because each must follow the other.

138

If we do not have that kind of mind developed to tackle a   566
situation, we will be bounced by blessing and tragedy,
tragedy and blessing, not knowing what is what. So, mentally, if we prepare ourselves that each follows the other and
live in an attitude of gratitude all the time, neither tragedies
will be tragedies for us, nor blessings will be blessings for us.
And in the end, all will be fair and final. That is known as
the constant state of consciousness, where man can live so
levitated that nothing matters to him. Remember, when
you are too happy, your heart can fail; when you are too
sad, your heart can fail.

Be enlightened that the other human being is you.   567
Understand through compassion that passion will make you
misunderstand. Vibrate on the cosmos and the cosmos will
clear your path. When fear and insecurity leave you, truth
and spirit will be with you.

Those who are humble in practice are always righteous in   568
the face of God. They are protected by the Supreme Being
and shall always live in plentiful abundance.

What can you do for the man who in happiness forgets   569
God, and in anger and rage is not afraid of God? In reality,
God is nothing but infinity and the origin of the man starts in
infinity and ends in infinity. It is this transition period
where you have come to go; not recognizing that we have
come to go is the source of the problem.

A freeway has lanes but within that freeway there are four   570
lanes. You can't make a fifth lane. The moment you try to
become a master of a fifth lane, you get off the freeway.
This is the play of ego, the individual personality, within the
confines of Infinite Will. In the expression of one's own
psyche, when ego makes a man overproject himself, in any
field, he goes off the track. Ego is an essential part of the
human psyche, but it has to be in balance, neither too
much of it nor too little of it is right.

What is higher consciousness and what is lower con-   571
sciousness? Anything which relates to self at the cost of
others is lower consciousness. Anything where self is
sacrificed for the cost of others is higher consciousness.

How many times do you keep yourself from God-   572
consciousness when you try to pretend you are great and
holy and you try to shield that negative part of you?

In my consciousness there is a support and in the support   573
there is an equal negative and an equal positive. There are
always two balances in each personality which balances the
very rhythm of life.

Learn to exist in the state of nonexistence; that is reality.   574

Neither an appearance is bad nor an act is bad; it is a bad   575
intention which is the problem. And what are the bad intentions? Cunning devices.

A person who cannot discuss his higher self with his lower self and his lower self with his higher self has a great subconscious problem.

Devotion

The only thing that pays in your life is patience. I used to   577
see in my active life that one who hasn't got patience is a
patient. The highest test of the human being is whether he
has patience or not.

In the beginning there was a longing; longing was God and   578
longing is God.

In the beginning there was a communion; communion was   579
with God, communion was God.

In the beginning there was a desire; desire was with God,   580
desire was God.

When you fold hands, you neutralize yourself 581
energywise, and when you bow, your whole blood circulation goes toward the head. When the magnetic field is
neutral and the circulation goes to the head, the brain func-
tions very well, even the dullest brain starts, becomes bright
and active; that's why in India, it was a custom that when
you went to meet your great master or guru or beloved
yogi, it was customary to bow to him and it was customary
until he tapped on your back that you did not lift your head.
What the great gurus used to do was when somebody came
and bowed to them, they would take a friend and go on a
long walk, and come back after six hours. If the person was
still there, they would come and tap his back. They would
say, "How are you?" He would say, "I am enlightened."
Naturally, six hours, six hours in that position could
enlighten a dead person.

Someone asked me once in a class, "What should one not 582
lose?" I said, "One's innocence. The highest prized quality
is one's own innocence. No matter how clever and
diplomatic and shrewd and intellectually creative you are,
you are basically nothing because the beauty of the man lies
in his innocence."

If you rise in the primal hours and always meditate on the 583
primal word, you will always be honored. You will see
liberation happening to you in life. Nanak* knew this is the
way you can become truth and truth can become you.

*Guru Nanak, the founder of Sikh Dharma and first in
line of the Ten Sikh Gurus

Don't follow Guru Nanak, be him; as he sang and exalted 584
God, you can do it in the same way. That is what he
showed us and he promised again and again. I am humble
of the humble, I am lowly of the low, I am meanest of the
mean, O Lord, but look how you have exalted me that I
can sing those praises for you which are even strange to
me.

The most difficult thing on the earth one can practice is to 585
be humble. It is not easy; it is difficult, because you have to
surmount the existence of whole maya and to recognize
that God is by your side. Then you feel the humility.

God guarantees that those who serve with devotion will 586
go across this world ocean.

I have a Father and He has a heaven and you can reach 587
Him my way. I am the only way. If you have the compassion which I have, if you have the love which I have, if you
have the humility which I have, if you have the service
which I have, surely as I go to the house of my Father, the
kingdom of my Father, you go too; and there is no other
way than that way. I have to be like that to go, and you
have to be like that also.

When there is a holy man and you touch his feet, what 588
can he do? What is left for him, except to say, "God bless
you." Right? If he has the habit of speaking the truth and if
he says God bless you, then God has to bless you. What
option has God?

Prayer is a control of the self in which you can talk to the   589
Infinite. In meditation God can talk to you and in prayer
you can talk to God.

Humility in action is universal consciousness.   590

If you have not risen above the five *tattwas** and have not   591
Christed yourself, why say you are Christian? How many of
you have walked in his footsteps? Try to understand first
who you are being with and then try to know how much
you have walked behind the master.

In the house of the Lord, progress is slow, but there is no   592
ultimate darkness. You shall be answered if you will call
Him.

Remember, everybody, for the sake of glory, has to carry   593
his own cross. That is the way the Lord made it by giving his
own personal example. He carried his own cross and he
asked for the terrible times and he got himself crucified for
your sins and laid an example by his sacrifice, that only by
getting the pain of others, you can ever, ever live in
pleasure.

*Earth, air, fire, water, and ether

I see you all in only one way. I see divine everywhere. Now 594
I have seen it, I cannot see anything else. If I am blind to the
man-made rules and regulations, that is not my fault. I have
lived under those rules and it was the grace and the glory of
the Master who gave me sight; now I have that sight and I
don't want to lose it at any cost; I am more willing to lose
this body, this vehicle, and leave it here, then to lose that
sight which has taken me beyond time, beyond karmas.

Sacrifice is the beginning of every love; we all know about 595
it, but we do not practice it. To subject yourself is to receive
the object, but how many can subject themselves?

It is fun to be selfish, but for higher values. I want to be 596
greedy so that I may be a really pious man. My greed is that
I should be a very good man. I am greedy to serve
everybody, I'm not greedy to be a disservice to people.

If you have the power to believe, then what you believe 597
shall come true. It means this little unit computer has the
power to organize the main Master Computer to act on a
signal. In simple rational words, man has control over the
Universal Consciousness. They call it *bhakti yoga*, also
devotion, worship.

The knot given by God can be opened by a man of God, 598
and the knot given by a man of God cannot be opened by
God.

Relationship

A teacher provides technical know-how; the disciple 599
masters it and becomes a great master—that is the law.
Those who adhere to this cosmic law and do the labor
become liberated.

What is a teacher? A teacher is a person who hammers 600
the egos and blends them into one.

Have faith in your own self because you are a self. 601
Nothing is beyond the self, nothing was beyond the self,
nothing shall be beyond the self, because you are a self in
the beginning and a self in the end; therefore, once you
realize the self you will be a realized self, then everything
will realize you.

By loving another human being and by merging your 602
identity, you learn to merge your identity into the total
cosmos; that is why a guru and a chela* come into relationship. Why do you need a guru? A guru is an individual, a
confined little thing into which an individual, a confined little
thing, totally merges his personality; then he exists with no
ego.

*Devotee or disciple

The job of the teacher is not to teach you the truth, 603
because you know the truth. You know the truth. The job
of the teacher is, out of his practical life and experience, to
remind you to live the truth. That's all it is. There is nothing
which you do not know.

When the object subjects itself, then subject and object 604
have no identity. When the slave merges into the master,
then the master and slave will have no difference;
therefore, every slave will end up as a master and every
master will end up as a slave, because every master will
become slave to the slave.

What is a human being? A magnetic field, that's all he is. 605
What kind of magnetic field is it? It vibrates on its own
nucleus and in proportion with its existence with the entire
universe. And there are many magnetic fields, millions of
them. Without your talking with somebody, you communicate.

Advice should be righteous, your mind should be 606
righteous, and your advice and activity to that advice
should be righteous. If a guru says, "Get up in the morning
and praise God," will you do it?
Answer: Yes.
Question: If the guru says "Get up in the morning and
steal," will you do it?
Answer: Yes.
Question: Is everything the guru says righteous?
Answer: Otherwise he is not a guru.
Question: Is it righteous to steal?
Answer: Perhaps he is testing, who knows. What is a
guru? A guru is an unknown infinity of you, otherwise
another human being cannot be a guru to you.

If there is a power to believe, to serve the people with compassion, whatever you were, whatever you are, you are holiest of the holy, if you have achieved a state of consciousness where you have compassion. God is a slave to people of compassion. 607

Some people acquire the habit of not admitting wrongs. 608
Admitting wrongs to one's own self is a chance for improvement. It is one of the highest virtues not because you will be judged by this world but you will be judged by your own higher consciousness. If you'll just feel and understand that you will become beneficial, you will become virtuous. Your judge is your own higher consciousness.

A man of dignity is also a man of universal ego; he gives 609
his head but doesn't bend.

Sometimes in our lives we do not value the values of such 610
values which can add values to our values.

Start understanding that you are the creative source and 611
nucleus of the whole vibratory effect. The moment you understand that, your problem is solved. The moment you know that you are you, your problems are over. The moment you know that you are you, God and you are one, because you are the Creator and He is the Creator.

If there is a purpose other than compassion in all relation- 612
ships in your life, you will also find pain in that relationship.

What is greatness? Greatness is when you have found 613
that you are not great, but everything else is. When everything else is great and you have experienced that, then
everything else holds you in its esteem.

We love the finite—the guru—to find the Infinite; and 614
that is the purpose of the guru, to give something to focus
on.

Great are those who have the company of the great 615
master, but greater still are those who live by the words of
the master, and they become great themselves.

There is no difference between you and me. He is speak- 616
ing and He is listening, and that is maya. If you understand
this maya, you will understand this whole truth. He is
speaking to me. He is listening to you, because He is the
giver of the breath. He gives me breath to speak and he
gives you breath to listen. If you understand this secret, you
understand everything.

In me, I have found only one reality—that I breathe in and 617
I breathe out. And so anything that breathes in or out is
reality. When I found this as a reality in everybody, I found
myself in everybody and everybody in myself.

There is a law of compassion that says, deal with the per- 618
son at his level of consciousness, amalgamate yourself at
that level of consciousness without having relation to yours,
and then pull him up. This law works in relationships and
friendships.

The third eye sees everything, the subconscious sees   619
everything. When you are in that ecstasy of coma of leaving
this earth and going to your home, it will tell you the whole
story in a very short time. It will show an entire movie. It will
show you all the players and all the extras in the cast. The
impact of the movie shall be such that you will have no face
to go to your Creator. A shameful man cannot go home. A
man who has broken the tradition and expectation of the
parents cannot enter the door of the home. Parents may be
longing to see him, but he does not go because he does not
feel himself worthy.

In any relationship, when there is any desire or exploitation   620
involved, this relationship is known as living *at* someone.
Living *with* people is when you join forces with people to inspire other people toward happiness. Living *for* people is
when you are willing to sacrifice your material, mental, and
energetic spiritual strength to raise and elevate another
man. These are the three types of relationships. The third
type which makes you live for other people makes you immortal, the second type of relationship makes you happy,
the first kind of relationship makes you miserable. And this
pattern of behavior decides our destiny.

The relationship between the cosmos and the individual,   621
and the individual and the individual, is exactly the same
relationship because everybody has his own cosmos. If one
does not know to relate in relationship to another person's
total cosmos existence, you cannot establish any relationship whatsoever.

Our relationships are based on three things: money, the 622
media (because they can hire and fire), the woman (the
regenerative instinct of the man). That is why woman is
very powerful to the man and vice versa; the man wants to
control and rule people. So these are the three basic things
which push a man ahead. But there is a relationship above
these three things and that is that you see the soul and
divinity in everybody and meet everyone on the level of
soul to soul.

Start thinking right and you will become right. And that 623
thinking about how much right I am or how much wrong
decides how near or far you are from God. If you feel you
are wrong, you also feel you are away from God. If you feel
right, then you also feel very near to God. There is no
distance between you and God; it is your thinking that puts
you at a distance.

Is anybody under his own control? Are you here because 624
of me? And am I here because of you? No. It is the Will of
the One to be one with everyone and so He wills and so He
desires and so He gets and prevails. Nobody belongs to
anybody and nobody doesn't belong to anybody. All
belong to the One.

Giving is a principle and it is an everlasting principle. Your 625
Creator gave you life and that is why he is the great Giver.

Our subconscious is so clogged that we normally choose 626
three things incorrectly: wife, profession, and friends.

No man is a perfect master, none. The only one perfect 627
master that a man of God can experience is God himself.

The relationship between the disciple and the guru is es- 628
tablished at that stage when the disciple realizes the ecstasy
of infinity.

It doesn't take time to open your heart and to feel the love 629
in you. But when will you do it? That is what takes time.

A clarity of mind brings compassion in the heart. Com- 630
passion in the heart brings Godlike acts, and Godlike acts
bring the readiness and capacity of God in you.

My job is to share with you knowledge. Your job is to 631
practice, to experience the knowledge, so that it may
become your knowledge.

What you relate to, that you shall be. Actually, you are 632
immortal. You are a consciousness.

Ignoring your soul is ignoring your Godhead; as a rose has 633
an aroma, so you have a soul; as a mirror has an image, so
you have a soul. Ignoring your soul is ignoring your total
capacity.

If you in your behavior and activity relate only on a 634
physical level, you are acting on a very gross level. If in your
behavior and activity you are only applying your mind, you
are using your intellect. But if in your existence and behavior, you apply the very fundamental soul of you, you become a universal consciousness.

No two bodies are alike and no two minds are alike. What 635
is alike? The spirit, the soul.

Meditation is your creativity and your activity in relation- 636
ship to the existence of the cosmos. It is the individual harmony in relationship to the universal harmony in existence.
And as strong as that meditation is, that strong the harmony
is.

There is one way you can always tell a man of God; talk to 637
him and he will talk the language of infinity. In half an
hour's talk you can measure and gauge the man very completely. Talk to him about the world, its successes or
failures. In the end he will lead you to one thing, that the
total creation is created by the Creator and we are part of
that infinity.

A guru is like an ocean where you can totally merge your- 638
self and come out washed and clean. A guru is the secret
chamber of your inner self where you can confine your
greatest secret and be guided to the secret light of
righteousness.

We cannot discuss what is good and what is bad for 639 somebody, but everybody has a level of consciousness. In other words, you have a horizon, a limit that you can see. Go higher and higher and higher, a big place will become smaller and smaller and smaller; ultimately, it will look like a dot to you, and then finally it will vanish the higher you go in consciousness. A likeness comes; we are alike, all souls are alike.

A guru is a guide. He is a guide, not a director. Guidance 640 is when you suggest the truth and do not attach with it. You will go to him and tell him your problem. He will suggest to you, under the given circumstances, what righteousness is. It is up to you to do it or not because you are also a God-conscious human being.

Many avatars came. They came and claimed that God is 641 right in them. I agree. I want to know who that person is in whom God is not.

Your body is given to you for payment of karma on this 642 planet. Whatever you are it is your karma, but you can change your entire destiny if you relate to infinity; I am a human being, God is with me and everything will be all right. It is not a question of belief, it is a question of practice, and it has nothing to do with changing your religion or changing your name; that is not required. It is the self built in. Whenever you vibrate that you are a creation of the Creator, then the Creator has to stand by you.

All souls are alike. Let's take the example of the army. 643
There are fifty privates. What is the position of each private?
Somebody is the gunner, somebody is the tank man,
somebody may just be a sweeper, someone else is an
orderly. The fifty people have different jobs, but in the army
they all are privates. Exactly in the same way, a soul has an
assigned karma and that soul has an infinite relationship
with the Supreme Consciousness.

Whatever you say is a mantra. Whatever you say is being 644
recorded and on that will be decided your credit and balance. Your mental and physical vibration reflect your soul
and there is no such thing as negativity. Negativity is when
either you are not communicating or another party is not
communicating. The problem is that the relay sinks the
ship; this equals no relationship. The relay communicates,
so if there is a friend, keep the frequency at a positive channel. Even if one is your enemy, then keep your positivity.

If man can awaken himself to the awareness that he is a 645
man, then his destiny changes. What you must know in
your life is that you are positively a human being.

A child is born to you to help him face his karma in this 646
life. A child is not your ego, it is not a pet dog in the house,
it is not a substitute for love. A child has nothing to do with
that. A child is born to you so that you can prepare him to
face time unto infinity.

Individual consciousness will refine you, group conscious- 647
ness will expand you, and universal consciousness will
redeem you to infinity.

Man as a creator is so much dependent on his Creator 648 that you cannot believe it. And sometimes when you are dependent on something, you don't like it, so you become atheistic. We don't like to feel we are dependent on anything. We don't like the idea of God. It is just like a tractor that doesn't like the driver; it just wants to run itself.

If a man knows his value, the whole world will value him. If 649 a man knows his value, he speaks the truth and his words become the truth. A teacher is one who knows you and reminds you of your value.

If you get into the stage of ecstasy, the Wha state, you can 650 overcome anything; all handicaps and problems in your life shall stand covered and you will have a bridge. You have to build this bridge. Nobody can build the bridge for you and that bridge is to train your mind. When as a human being I know the being of the being, time is here and now and to-morrow I shall be all right.

The difference between you and an animal is that the 651 animal has limited compassion and you can have unlimited compassion.

A man of God speaks the truth, enlightens people, raises 652 their consciousness. So people follow him, like him, love him. Their mind is affected, their mind affects their children. Generation to generation, on it goes.

You must live in group-consciousness and you must prac- 653 tice universality. It will lead you to righteousness. It will lead you to grace. It will lead you to God-consciousness.

You all know the truth. If you think you can learn what the 654
truth is or what righteous living is, you are mistaken. You all
know what righteous living is and what truth is. Everybody
knows it, but we can't live up to it; some of us do not want
to live up to it. Now, the question is why can't we live up to
it? We are emotionally involved with each other. When our
emotional involvement seems absolutely perfect, it is very
difficult for any one of us to pull ourself out of it. And when
you are not out of the mud, how can you see what you are
doing?

Why find God? Where is God? Is He on holiday? 655
Whatever happened to Him? If you realize that God is omniscient, omnipresent, and omnipotent, then you must forget finding Him. You have already found Him. He is in you
and you are in Him. But if you have no real connection with
Him in that way, then keep on searching and I can guar-
antee that you will never find Him.

There is nothing wrong with having a good car, an 656
airplane, a boat, a twenty-room house. There is nothing
wrong with it. If you have it you are blessed. Have
everything but don't be concerned (attached) with it. It is
absolutely all right to have six cars. No problem. But don't
be concerned about such things. Material concerns can
sometimes take the form of disease, a sickness.

When I see the sun, it doesn't want liberation, neither has 657
the moon ever tried for it, neither do the stars seek it. I see
them so wonderfully beautiful, so organized in their being,
so one-pointed in their consciousness, that I sit back in my
tiny self and I call it *Wha, Wha,* many times. He is all
around everywhere, through each one. Then, I see every
molecule in me, around me, is nothing but a teacher.

I don't think anybody has to learn what the truth is. 658
Everybody knows the truth. All man does need to learn is
how to live the truth. And when he lives the truth, he
becomes the truth.

The Creator creates people to become nothing but mirrors 659
into which He can look and see in them their own defects
and their own effects in existence.

Religion is a method whereby a man of achieved con- 660
sciousness can make another man his own original consciousness. It doesn't matter if you are a Christian, it doesn't
matter if you are a Buddhist, it doesn't matter if you are a
Jew. I don't find any difference. Suppose we are to reach
Tokyo, Japan. Does it matter which airline we take so long
as the airline can take us to Tokyo?

Everything in this universe has been created as a teacher. 661
The moon is a teacher, the sun is a teacher, the stars are a
teacher. But there are people who become professional
reminders. That is what we call a teacher. A teacher is a
professional reminder.

A teacher is a professional person reminding the man to 662
realize that he belongs in the finite to the infinity.

What we are trying to do is not to live at each other, not 663
to live with each other, but to live for each other.

RELATIONSHIP

Exactly as a person on this earth does not understand the   664
relationship between the male and the female, in the same
way the creation does not understand the relationship between God and maya.

Without a guru, everywhere is darkness. Now where is   665
that guru? Does he hold a lantern in his hand? No. The guru
is one who guides you. The technique of the guru is with
you for practice and availability. The guru is that wisdom
which you have attained and which you experience within
when you overcome adversaries, when the body and mind
are on one side and your higher self is on one side.

Consciously you must be conscious that nobody is wrong;   666
therefore, you must not slander anybody. When you
slander other people, actually your consciousness goes
from a higher level to a lower level.

Between two people there is a God; among three, a   667
whole government.

Selfishness is not when you make a hundred dollars and   668
you want three hundred dollars. Selfishness is when you
want at your state of consciousness and when you are not
willing to accommodate another man in his state of consciousness. That is selfishness.

The essence of life is the essence of life and you must   669
create the creativity of life with certain values. There is no
other beauty in a man other than his values.

166

Whether I am a male or a female, I am high or low, I am poor or rich, I am white or black, I am an existence, and there is some cause somewhere for my existence. And my existence which has a cause must have an effect, because cause must have an effect; then why I should subject myself to anyone except my cause? And my cause is Infinity, and so I must subject myself to Infinity. 670

It is the first thankless job of the teacher to create environments which the student cannot understand right away. If the student understands right away, he will just go through it. The teacher should be intelligent enough to create a problem which the student does not understand and then he should push the student through it and that will bring faith. This faith will move mountains and those mountains will move God. The formless will fade behind form the way cats fade behind cows. 671

There is one way only to reach a higher consciousness. There can be many trips, but there is only one way. And that is the way of righteous living. There is no other way, every other way will be hanky-panky. But the moment you decide, come what may, I am going to give myself to the way of righteousness within me, you will be surprised to see that everything else in this whole world will fall in place for you. Because when the psyche, the nucleus of the psyche, creates the magnetic field of the opposite energy in relevance to all relationship of the universal energy, then the entire magnetic field rotates in that rhythmic self. 672

Techniques

There are no accidents. Anything that comes to you, you   673
have put out beams for it.

Kundalini yoga is the science of angles and triangles.   674

There are eight staircases leading to the peaks of the   675
mountains. The top of the mountain represents the higher
self, and the staircase, the genuine path of the being.
Underneath is written: Ek Ong Kar Sat Nam Siri Wha Guru!

Teaching is not a verbalization or a communication;   676
teaching is also not a direction; teaching is to be.

Is yoga a religion? It is and it is not. In religion you have to   677
believe something and in yoga you have to experience what
you want to believe.

There are many kinds of yoga and in the West we have   678
many thoughts about them, but as far as kundalini yoga is
concerned, it is the yoga of awareness. The total potential
of the person becomes known to the person. Every known
has an unknown potential and that unknown potential is
your right to know. Why don't you know? Because you do
not have the technical know-how and that technical know-
how is available to the man through the learned great
teachers who have left that for us.

In kundalini yoga we don't worry about the effect, we   679
worry about the cause, because cause has the effect. Effect
can never happen without cause; consequences shall never
happen without sequence. If a person can be aware enough
to know the trend of the sequences, he can control the consequences.

If you can master the nine gates of your body—eyes, ears,   680
nose, mouth, sex organ, and rectum—then all of the se-
crets of nature will open to you.

When the ego merges with the soul, then a person is   681
enlightened. The moment the ego dies, it is death; we call it
Maha Samadhi. You know the dos and don'ts; physical exercises, asanas; pranayama exercises; then concentration,
contemplation, meditation, and then absorption, *samadhi*.
Maha Samadhi, great absorption, means death. In India we
don't write that anybody has died, we say he has gone into
Maha Samadhi.

When we chant a name, we create a special heat in 682
which all of the karmas get burned and we become
neutralized.

Your life always changes in seven years. Within seven 683
years your loss must turn into a gain and your gain must
turn into a loss. That is how this universe has been created.
This is a cosmic cycle.

Who is powerful, God or you? When you do the *japa*, 684
chanting repetitiously, then the result is *tapa,* the heat that
burns the karma.

People vibrate with a given physical energy. When the 685
given physical energy vibrates and exalts the Infinite Word,
then mental energy correlates and universal energy takes
over.

Somebody asked me, "If I go for ten years to learn from a 686
Zen Master, what will he teach me?" I said, "He will teach
you how to sit, that's all. In that you will have all the
knowledge of the universe. If you learn how to sit, then you
know how to stand and then you know how to walk and
then you know how to talk and then you know how to communicate and then you can produce anything and destroy
anything you like."

Kundalini yoga is a method to become nothing, so that 687
everything can flow through you. That's all it is.

Mantra has no meaning unless you have the meter of it. 688
The moment you know how to play an instrument, music
will come out of it.

It can never be that all will have the same thing. This is im- 689
possible. You may find socialism, communism, or
capitalism, but everyone cannot have everything. And
why? No individual has the same aura; therefore, no individual has the same magnetic field; therefore, no attraction will be the same. So, you can't have the same thing.

The body has been given to me to realize and I must 690
realize while I am in the body. I am not talking in mystical
terms. When the vibratory nucleus realizes that the
magnetic field of its own psyche is in relationship to the
magnetic field of the universal psyche, this creates a harmony, and then the merger is with Infinity.

All human beings intuitively know what is going on. The 691
difference is, some can record it and some cannot. In simple words, we can say that everybody has a tape recorder,
but some are without tape and some have tape. Those who
have tape can tape-record and those who don't cannot
record.

To be aware who you are is an awareness, and if this 692
awareness, your self-awareness, can relate to the universal
awareness, there is an absolute harmony. Then you are a
yogi.

Samskaras are the karmas of the past life. Your shape of 693
body and the opportunity which comes to you are your
samskaras. If man is not solid with faith within himself, he is
more affected by samskaras than by karmas.

Karma is Newton's third law. Buddha got enlightened 694
with Newton's third law: Every action has a reaction, equal
and opposite.

What is meditation? When you empty yourself and let the 695
universe come in you.

Kriya means action—an action which must sprout the 696
seed.

The soul is the contact unit of the inflow and outlet of in- 697
finity. Some say the soul is in the heart, some say the soul is
in the solar plexus, some say it is in the brain. But do you
know where the soul is? It is the circumvent force around
the body, which mystics call the arc of life. Aura is the outer
projection and arc is the inner projection. The arc is the
point of contact between the astral body and the gross
body.

What is Christ-consciousness called? We call it kundalini, 698
when man uncoils his potential in activity.

Creative meditation is the situation in which man can 699
create the environments in which man can speak to man.

Group-consciousness is an intermediate stage. It is what   700
you pass through in the journey from individual consciousness to universal consciousness.

The yogi is one who has a union with his Supreme Con-   701
sciousness. If flexibility of the body is the only yoga, then
clowns in the circus are the best yogis.

Why does the teacher sit higher than the student? The   702
student studies from the sixth center, *ajna,* the forehead,
the humility; and the teacher teaches from the heart center,
the fourth center, the compassion, and projects the truth
from the fifth center, the throat.

No man can escape physical death. Whosoever is born   703
must die. The great mistake is that man starts worshipping
man instead of worshipping Infinity, which he must worship
and understand through knowledge. You can respect me,
love me, cater to me, and I can give you all the technical
wisdom, but you have to experience the knowledge, and
that will be when, on a level of creativity, you experience it
through practice.

What is intuition? Intuition is a relationship. Intuition is   704
the recording of a vibratory unit in relation to your existence, that's all.

The conscious regulation of the breath is to bring about a   705
balance of energy in the nervous system.

Life is not given to us to live as a routine. It is given to us   706
as our destiny. It is given so we experience life. Every day
we must die and we must experience that death. And every
day we must be reborn and must experience resurrection.

What is kundalini? The energy of the glandular system   707
combines with the nervous system to become more sensitive so that the totality of the brain perceives signals and
interprets them, so that the effect of the sequence of the
cause becomes very clear to the man. In other words, man
becomes totally, wholesomely aware. That is why we call it
the yoga of awareness. And as the rivers end up in the
same ocean, all yoga ends up by raising the kundalini in the
man. What is the kundalini? The creative potential of the
man.

There is no one good or bad, only your actions have an ef-   708
fect that is equal and opposite. You cannot get away from
Newton's third law.

If you want to get out of your karma, there is only one way,   709
vibrate the Nam. The Nam is the vibration of the praise of
Infinity.

Every word uttered by you must come back to you within   710
twelve years and it must grip you within the scale of seven
years. This is a law of nature.

May your guru and your God stand by you, may the 711
realms of all angels bless you, may the purity of your heart
stand by you, may your divine nature help you, and may
your God-consciousness lead you.

O my mind, practice yoga in this way. Eat as much as you 712
can digest and eliminate, light food. Sleep as if it were a
nap. Kindness, mercy, and forgiveness should be your
practice. The man who does this will not have to find God,
for God will find him.

One of the three kinds of garbage that we put in our body 713
is physical dirt. You should never overfeed yourself,
because the body has to work overtime to eliminate it. Eat
to live, don't live to eat.

Nobody can speak the infinite truth until the plate of the 714
mind is clear. And what we offer is technical know-how to
rub the plate of the mind and make it shiny and clear.

He whom the Creator has blessed with the gift of 715
tolerance and nonreaction is the most blessed one. For do
you know when you don't react you are immediately identified as a God? When you react you are known. When you
don't react you are unknown. If you are trying to find the
Unknown, all you have to do is not react. There is only one
simple thing you have to practice: Do not react.

Patience gives you the power to practice; practice gives 716
you power that leads you to perfection.

I am" is not the complete mantra. It must be, "I am, I   717
am." "I am" is the finite and "I am" is the infinite and the
mind must shuttle between the two.

What is prayer? You create a vibratory effect which goes   718
into the Infinite Creative around the psyche of you. The
answer and energy come and then your job is done and
your prayer has worked.

The first act of surrendering to God is to live as He has   719
made you. The second act of surrendering to God is to
maintain what hair God has given you on the crown of your
head. The third act of sacrifice is to meditate on the five
primal sounds in the morning and praise the Lord before
the sun rises.

Creative meditation is that every moment you exist as a   720
part of the universe, the whole universe becomes a part of
you.

There are stages of realization: Guru, Sat Guru, Siri Guru,   721
and Wha Guru. And Wha Guru is God Himself. There is
only one Siri Guru, the Siri Guru Granth. There are many
Sat Gurus. Sat Guru is the level of truth, the complete truth
in the consciousness of the individual. Guru is the level of
consciousness when you apply the formula. Guru means
when you bring the light. Guru means one who applies the
formula of that light. Sat Guru is one who experiences that
formula through which he experiences the light. Siri Guru is
one who is ever constant in that light. Wha Guru is that
ecstasy of Infinity.

Here is a life schedule. For the first twenty-five years, gain   722
knowledge; for the second twenty-five years, experience
that knowledge in existence with humility in the grace of the
self in relation to the creativity of the Universal Infinity,
which means in one word, God; for the third twenty-five
years, spread and share; for the last twenty-five years, get
ready to go. That covers one hundred years and if death
comes earlier, great. The earlier, the better.

If the rhythm of the breath with the mantra will not relate to   723
the rhythm of the mind, the mantra will not work. That is
the secret.

Tantric is the science of point, of *bindu*. No science is more   724
absolute. Tantric means the width and the length, the
longitude and the latitude. Everything has a length and a
breadth. And every length and breadth comes out of point,
bindu. And tantric has a trinity—black, red, and white.
Spirituality has three dimensions—the black, the red, and
the white. When you talk about the black dimension, you
talk about when you scare people with spiritual powers and
try to control them. That is black magic. Red magic is when
you demonstrate miracles; you do this to show off and con-
vince people. White is when you live humbly, universally,
radiantly, truthfully, so that when one sees you, one sees
God through you.

The living trinity is to know the truth, to practice the truth,   725
and to sacrifice for the truth; and if it means death, you are
willing to die. We call it the trinity of attitude, and the word
samadhi means attitude.

Meditation on breath is a meditation on life. It is very simple. This sound in you is an infinite sound and so long as this sound of inhale and exhale continues, you are alive. They call it *Anhat*, ultimate mantra. If you don't chant this mantra, you cannot chant any others either. You have to chant this mantra in every religion before every God. Any moment that you cannot chant this mantra, you cannot exist. Do it gracefully, rhythmically, and musically. It is known as *pranayam*, and it is very essential.   726

Whatever name of God you want to chant, just do it. It will tune you in. It will be your own biofeedback machine.   727

Man has to reach the state of awakened sleep, which they call *turia* state of mind. Turia state of mind is when you know the unknown of the individual as well as the state of the universe.   728

Meditation is when the mind is totally clean and receptive and God talks to the man.   729

Without creative meditation a man will feel burdened; the law of detachment does not become functional in the man if he is not creative.   730

You can't live without meditation. Imagination and activity, with emotions and commotions, when these are blended with the steering of the personality, that's what meditation is. You relate your unit activity toward the Infinity, and the question is, are you creative or uncreative? This will decide your train of life.   731

Some people think that this is meditation: For twenty   732
minutes you sit on the chair, *Sat, Sat Nam, Om, God,
Jesus.* Or you sit on a mat with your back straight. You
think this is meditation, but it is not meditation. It is an effort
to try to prepare yourself for meditation. Preparation is not
the complete result.

You may have heard of transcendental meditation and   733
integral meditation; there are many labels. Just as there are
for mustard seed: yellow mustard seed, sunflower mustard
seed, Sun Valley mustard seed, California mustard seed,
Wisconsin mustard seed, New York mustard seed; mustard
seed is mustard seed. Similarly, different techniques of
yoga have been given different names. Hatha yoga has the
same end: to raise the kundalini in a person. Raja yoga has
the same end. Bhakti, shakti, gian, karma yoga—all have
the same end, to raise the dormant power of infinity in the
man; that's all.

There are two ways of earning a universal consciousness.   734
One is through hardship; the other is an easy way—mantra.
But there is difficulty with mantra yoga. Relating the mantra
to the Infinite Being and the finite, and creating that direct
connection, opens up the heart magically, but to have the
mental fluctuation for that capacity is a little difficult.

Concentrate on this mantra—*Wha, I am the great spirit.* It   735
will bring fulfillment and good luck.

A common soul frees itself from the earth attachment in   736
seventeen days after death.

The magnetic field on which the current of life runs computes thought waves and it is connected with the Supreme Computer; this is known as destiny. 737

One guru will not suit everybody. All minds are different. There are three minds: the gunas—sattwa, rajas, and tamas. A person who by habit is a guru shall cater to all these three gunas at the level of that guna. A guru will come to the level required and still be a guru. A guru is the most flexible man. He must cater at every level because he is a channel through which wisdom flows; therefore, his channel must fit in everywhere. 738

A guru can be a word of wisdom coming through a person who has attained a state of mental consciousness to direct or guide or speak the infinite truth under all circumstances. 739

The physical body is a temple. Take care of it. The mind is energy. Regulate it. The soul is the projection. Represent it. All knowledge is false if the soul is not experienced in the body. 740

Activity with responsibility, honesty, and self-consciousness leads to God-consciousness. That is karma yoga. 741

Temperamentally, man is a very undisciplined animal; the highest achievement is when he disciplines himself. 742

Mantra is what? Man's protection. And man's protection 743
lies in what? In existence; righteous existence leads to man's
protection.

You must leave your limitations and use all methods to 744
raise your consciousness. If you understand kundalini, you
understand the whole universe. It is your existence. It is the
power in you through which you make your mind expand.

If your heart is clean, your consciousness is clean, and then 745
if you are slandered, you are liberated. That slander is
washing our karma.

Be loved for your knowledge, your experience, and your 746
faith.

First is the mother, Guru Dev Mata. Then there is the 747
father, Guru Dev. All relationships teach us a lot. And then
there is the final guru, who teaches you and pushes you
toward Infinity.

The fundamental awareness is the fundamental uncoiling 748
of oneself, the kundalini. What is kundalini? It is not a ser-
pent power. Kundalini means kundal. Kundal means lock
of the beloved's hair. Uncoiling the coil within yourself, that
is what kundalini means—the energy to be uncoiled.

The definition of personality is the particular stream-of- 749
thought patterns.

Who is a Buddhist? The one who has the *buddhi*, the eye 750
to see the Omnipresent in everything.

There are five elements of which man is made. These five 751
elements have five desires and the five desires pull the man
down The five elements are ether, air, earth, water, and
fire. The elements have ego, anger, greed, attachment, and
lust. How can man come out of it? If he Christs himself.

Feel that you exist, then turn yourself into a star. This is a 752
very powerful meditation. Feel your body entirely, from toe
to top, then feel your body totally as a star; then emit the
shine. You are turning yourself into a star. Project a lot of
light, then become separate from it and watch it.

We say and we know the truth but we do not practice it to 753
the point of perfection. We must practice truth with a sense
of perfection so that no one will be in a position to take us
away from it.

Why in old age are we frustrated? Because there is not a 754
lot of wisdom for us to share. The only value in old age is
wisdom. So, in your life train your mind with the
knowledge of perfect harmony in every relationship. Communicate freely and learn from everything the art of living.
This, the highest art of this planet, must be mastered so that
you can live realized.

Dear ones, there are assets and there are liabilities. When 755
you are young, you need food. If food is not available, you
feel crazy. When you are adult, sex becomes the grip. If you
don't have satisfaction in that area, you go crazy. But when
you are old, wisdom is your grip. If you don't have wisdom
in your head, you are crazy. These three eras are covered
by these three assets.

If we all had to die for our mistakes, none of us would be 756
alive. We commit mistakes every day. But there is a protective hand around us all the time. It is life's magnetic field,
the psyche of individual existence. The psyche of individual
existence creates a magnetic field in which the vibratory
level must keep itself on channel and in tune; and that is
why we are above, although we are in the physical form.

When we know we are Infinity, why can we not function 757
as that? This is a great question. When we know we are
That, why are we not in that consciousness? Why do we
slip? Lack of training, that is why we slip. As the ordinary
man climbs a mountain, he will slip; but one who is trained
in mountaineering and has educated himself in the art of
mountaineering will not slip. Therefore, a man has to be
trained in the art to be a man. A human being has to be
trained in the art of being a human being. If a person is not
trained in the art to mentally be, a slip is inevitable.

Meditation is something that can make you understand 758
that you have been living an uneasy life. When you
meditate, all uneasiness, which is physical and mental,
must appear. Meditation is a mental cleansing. Good
meditation is when all the garbage comes out. All that
comes in meditation is then cleaned out.

B etween you and God, between you the creature and the   759
Creator there is only one link, and that is the breath of life.

W hen man leaves this earth, with him goes nothing but   760
his will, his inspiration, and his consciousness; his aim and
his object; what he looks at as a being.

Y ou have to transmigrate your existing being to a nonex-   761
isting being.

T he effect of Sa Ta Na Ma* is that your existence becomes   762
truth with the relative existence of the universe.

I t is not possible that you will not create anything because   763
you are a vibration; therefore, you must vibrate, and your
vibration will create an action and reaction in relation to the
universal vibration.

T hese are four states of awareness: awake state, dream   764
state, deep sleep state, and deep sleep aware state. These
are the four stages of mental activity.

I will tell you the difference between psychic power and in-   765
tuitional power. Intuitional power is a battery which works
on the cosmic energy which is given by the solar center.
Psychic power is a battery which works on the individual
electricity, individual energy.

*See introduction for explanation.

Every seventy-two hours you change your physical self; 766
all cells in your body within seventy-two hours must
change. What you are now in seventy-two hours you will
not be in the next seventy-two hours; you will be a completely different person.

Your body is in a protective field which we call a circum- 767
vent force. It is the eighth center of the human body. It is
around you and it communicates between the universal
energy and your individual existence. When the outward
vibrations are effectively negative, it transmits a signal to the
inner protective self for steadiness and for stationary existence. That is why, at that time, mentally man does not
want to move.

Your electromagnetic field, which is responsible for your 768
silent communication in this universe, centers on your
spine. If you do not know how to sit straight you do not
know how to live straight and nothing will go right and
straight in your life.

We all have something in common. We all breathe, 769
therefore we all vibrate and that vibration is the source of
our life. Whosoever can create rhythm within his own vibration, the entire creation will create a rhythmic sound around
him.

Talk or philosophy will open you to new dimensions of 770
your life. Physical exercise will open you to new dimensions, and meditation will open you to new spheres of consciousness.

There are eighty-four postures of yoga, but both the 771 Westerner and the Easterner have done it in the womb of the mother, so you are yogis anyway.

When a man becomes a man, he gets a hue around him; 772 then the center is fixed.

Action has a reaction equal and opposite; this is Newton's 773 law, which nobody should forget. If you eat more, you have indigestion. Whatever you do, you will be paid in equal terms; but when you subject your free will in the Will of the Lord the Creator, He will love you more than you expect Him to love. He will love you tenfold.

There are two ways to find the Divine. One way is to open 774 the solar plexus, totally charge your solar centers, and you become direct with the Divine. The other way is that you concentrate and meditate and you get this sound in you; thus it directly charges your solar center and you get the Divine light. This sound is a precise sound. Ek Ong Kar Sat Nam Siri Wha Guru!

Without a guru there is a darkness; one cannot be 775 liberated without a guru, a guide. Until we have a con- firmed habit to remind ourselves, we need a sentry, we need training. Until we graduate, we go to college.

A guru, a teacher, a messiah, a master is a technical 776 know-how man. If it doesn't work for you, find another technique; and if that doesn't work, find another technique. Every part doesn't fit every car.

Here are the following stages of the development of man: 777
First you want to know; after knowing, you want to acquire;
after acquiring, you want to master; after mastery, you
want to be recognized.

Every one of you is a radio. Simply switch on a frequency 778
and music will be heard; and that music will be heard by
your own conscious soul, and that will be your bliss and
happiness. Not only you but the surroundings of you will
become beautiful.

When a person mentally becomes so egocentric that he 779
does not want to hear what is happening in the totality, he
loses the greatest protective gift given to him. That is ex-
trasensory perception. We call it commonly the sixth sense.

There is a seen personality. This me is the seen personal- 780
ity; behind this personality there is a most important personality that is an unseen personality. Every seen must
have an unseen, every known must have its unknown.
Unknown is a God. Whenever I use the word God, I always
use it in the concept of a master computer. So, very scien-
tifically, a known must have its Unknown, a seen must have
its Unseen.

The first teacher is the mother; then the next teacher is the father; then the environment; and then God. When a person has devotion, his vibratory effect is totally exact. When the truth is totally exact or the vibratory effect is totally resolved into a complete surrender of receptivity, individuality becomes totality because everything is nothing but a consciousness, and consciousness cannot exist without vibration. Therefore, there is not consciousness without vibration.

There is a reality to be realized. I am infinity. I am not God, neither am I an accident of God. I am not this. I am not that. I am not now, I am not then. Who am I? I am a structure, I am a bunter. What is the structure about? It has a mantra vibration. Bunter has a mantra vibration; and that mantra must have a juntra, dimension; and juntra must have a tantra, nucleus; and tantra must have an untra, the essence, the realization. Now come bunter, munter, junter, tunter, and unter—five levels, five dimensions. This bunter must realize the unter: Sat Nam. Sat means truth, Nam means identity. The identity of this bunter is Sat; and how can it be expressed? By righteous living.

Through all the religions and languages, the knowledge giver has been defined in five ways. Guru means technical know-how. If you have technical know-how, you can share it with somebody, that is your job. That is my job. A guru is one who shares that technical know-how, the formula. Sat Guru is the one who truthfully, through compassion, watches the one sharing that formula. Normally we misunderstand that word. The Sat Guru is the one who has realized the truth. Sat Guru is the one who lets the student go through that truth by himself. Then comes Siri Guru, that title came to the word, Siri Guru Granth Sahib. All of the Gurus at that time took the language and truth of all that existed, bound them into a book and a word. The humanity started calling it Siri Guru because it is difficult to be a Siri Guru. As a human being, I have to express myself. Siri Guru does not express himself except in one way. It is the job of the Siri Guru to tell one thing in one way all of the time. That's why all scriptures are Siri Guru. They are the bound-down truth. Wha Guru is easy. You start with a guru and you end up with a guru on the human level, because the finite is connected with the Infinite. Breath is the secret.

Prayer

May his light be thy light. May his soul prevail, may his grace prevail and may this day go in conscious records to relate to the Supreme Consciousness. O Creator of this creation, create those environments to guide us on the path of righteousness, humility, truth, and love. Give us the power to give, give us the power to give, give us the power to give. Thy essence, O Lord, is giving, so that what you gave us, the infinity, we may give unto the infinity, to tilt the scale toward Thee, to find unto Thee happiness, love, and bliss.

Sat Nam